What's Inside

Finding the Right One in Light of the Beatitudes

by

Donald Thomas

fivesolaspress

Literature for your joy and God's glory

What's Inside
Finding the Right One in Light of the Beatitudes

by

Donald Thomas

Published by Five Solas Press
1084 Road 8
Powell, Wyoming 82435
www.fivesolaspress.com

Cover Design by Studio Gearbox (www.studiogearbox.com)
Edited by Greg S. Baker

ISBN-10: 0990937801
ISBN-13: 978-0990937807

First Edition

Library of Congress Cataloguing-in-Publication Data is on file at the
Library of Congress, Washington, D.C.
Library of Congress Control Number: 2014922789

Unless otherwise noted, all Scripture quotes are taken from
The Holy Bible, King James Version (KJV)

Scripture quotations marked *NASB* are taken from the *New American
Standard Bible,* © 1960, 1962, 1963, 1968, 1971, 1975, and 1977 by
The Lockman Foundation, La Habra, Calif. Used by permission.

Dedication

To my loving wife, Mary, who has been a God-given blessing and made our lives together a joy without measure. Her faithful devotion to Christ has enabled her to pass on the rich heritage of a virtuous wife and mother to our children and now our grandchildren.

To my children, Stephen, Julia, Lydia, Paul, Priscilla, Matthew, and Anna, who have taught me much about my God-entrusted responsibility of fatherhood through the crucible of the parenting experience. I love you very much!

Finally, to the young Christian singles that are pursuing God's will in whom they should marry, I dedicate this book to you. May God grace you with a marriage in Christ joyfully filled with His rich blessings. May God receive all the glory!

Contents

Acknowledgements

My appreciation extends to the elders and congregation of Trinity Bible Church who graciously gave me leave from the pulpit to pen these pages. I want to also acknowledge Gwen Kirk for her invaluable help and encouragement.

Preface

I began penning these words on the eve of the marriage of one of my daughters. Several years earlier, when all of my children were single and living at home, I began writing to them a series of letters to help guide them as they faced one of the biggest questions of their lives, "Who would God have me marry?" These letters developed into a sermon series entitled "Letters to My Kids," which I later shared with my Trinity church family.

As my children were growing up, my wife Mary and I faithfully prayed that God would bless each of them with a godly spouse, if it was His will that they marry. Like all parents, we longed that our children might enter into marriage unions that would bring lifelong blessings. There were times during family meals when we would ponder together God's plan for their lives with questions like, "I wonder where the person you will marry is living right now? What do you think he or she might be doing? Isn't it amazing that God is omniscient and He not only knows who that person is, but in His providence, He will one day intersect your lives?"

As an attorney and pastor, I was troubled by the high divorce rate among evangelicals which paralleled that of the unbelieving world. I had counseled and shed tears with many couples whose lives were shattered by marriages gone shipwrecked. Why is it that half of Christian marriages, which began with promise and joy on their wedding day, painfully end on the courthouse steps? Of course, there is no one simple answer, but the common thread that appeared to weave through many of these shattered marriages seemed to predate their wedding day. The problem lay in a defective thread found in the fabric of their courtship which preceded the marriage.

As a dad, I began to seek God's wisdom as to how I could help guide my children through the dangerous minefields of this selection process into God's pathway of blessing. My mind flooded with questions. Could it be that the world's approach to dating and marriage has infected the church? Has romantic comedy replaced God's Word as the model for finding a person to marry? Do the Scriptures point to a selection process for discovering God's will in marriage? How can you know if the person you are courting is Mr. or Mrs. Right?

The one common area that I observed Christian singles falling short in was the selection process itself. Many seemed to be pursuing the right person in the wrong way. If asked, I believe most single believers would say that they are praying that God might bring them a godly Christian spouse. However, they often fail to ask crucial follow-up questions like, "What does a godly Christian look like? How can you discern a person who's passionate about Christ?"

While I was preparing for a college Bible study on our Lord's Sermon on the Mount, my mind began to drift back to these questions about marriage. Could it be that many young singles are repeating the error common in David's day where man looked on the outward appearance, but the LORD looked on the heart (1 Samuel 16:7)? Is it possible that many young believers are confusing true godliness with nothing more than external, pharisaical religion?

Perhaps their eyes catch a handsome young man or an attractive young lady in a college Bible study. They are quick to notice that gold-initialed leather bound Bible in hand. They are excited to discover that their commitment is deeper than college meetings; they also faithfully attend the First Evangelical Church. When they later learn that this interesting person is also serving God by playing the keyboard during the worship service, they are absolutely certain that they have found their precious godly jewel. Because commitment is so rare today among professing Christians, it's tempting to confuse any outward religious activity with true conversion.

If you truly desire to marry a godly person, you must be willing to look behind their outward displays of religion into the deep recesses of their heart. Remember our Lord's sober warning, "Not every one that saith unto me, Lord, Lord, shall enter into the kingdom of heaven; but he that doeth the will of my Father which is in heaven. Many will say to me in that day, Lord, Lord, have we not prophesied in thy name? and in thy name have cast out devils? and in thy name done many wonderful works? And then will I profess unto them, I never knew you: depart from me, ye that work iniquity (Matthew 7:21-23).

How can you know the true nature of a person's spiritual heart? Ultimately, it's impossible to fully know your own heart let alone that of another person. Scripture warns us that "The heart is deceitful above all things, and desperately wicked: who can know it?" (Jeremiah 17:9). However, God has given us the stethoscope of His Word to listen for a spiritual heartbeat. Where there is a heartbeat, there is life!

In the Beatitudes—the truths that open our Lord's Sermon on the Mount—Jesus gives us eight heart attitudes found in all who have been saved by the grace of God. All eight of these character qualities will be present where God has imparted a new heart. Jesus tells us that these are the people who are eternally "blessed" or "happy." If you want a truly happy marriage, you must first become a happy person whose life bears the spiritual fruit found in the Beatitudes. You must then trust God to lead you to a happy person to marry. You will recognize that happy person as one who embodies all of the Beatitudes. As God joins two happy lives together in marriage, they become one in God's happiness!

My letters to my children were just one father's effort to guide his sons and daughters into this pathway of blessing. They were not intended to be a magic formula with guaranteed results. Rather, they were principles to help guide them in their walk of faith. It is my prayer that these letters might be helpful to other fathers and single Christians so that every unmarried man or woman who seeks a mate in the will of God can discover the right person that God might have them marry.

I write these pages first to parents—especially fathers. God has placed you in the important role of the spiritual head of your family. This role includes actively overseeing the courtship process of your children. It is my prayer that you might be men who faithfully labor for the souls and spiritual blessings of your sons and daughters. I would encourage you to go through these chapters with your children. Discuss with them their practical outworking in the life of your family. May our Lord equip and strengthen you for this high calling.

I write also to you who are unmarried with the prayer that God might, above all, continue to conform you into the image of His dear Son. Before you begin your pursuit of marriage, I encourage you to prayerfully apply each of these Beatitudes to your own life. Put the stethoscope of God's Word up to your own heart and make sure that God has graced you with the fruit of His salvation.

Perhaps the greatest test you will face in your pursuit of marriage will be to humbly bow your will to the express will of your Heavenly Father. Like Eve, you might be tempted by the seductive attraction of the outward appearance. Don't compromise! Keep tight reigns on your emotions that they don't run ahead of wise counsel and the prayerful discernment of the heart. Trust the wisdom of both your earthly and heavenly Fathers.

I will count it joy if the following chapters might become your companion and guide in discerning God's pathway to your happiness and His glory!

Chapter 1

A Fractured Tale

What therefore God hath joined together,
let not man put asunder.

- Matthew 19:6

It was my granddaughter's fourth birthday; the whole family was gathered in a circle to watch her eagerly open her presents. I quickly recognized the theme of her party: a princess theme complete with costume, cape, and a plastic sparkling crown fit for a most beautiful princess. Young girls love fairy tales where the beautiful girl always marries the handsome Prince Charming. Those fairy tales of our youth don't seem to lose their charm as we grow older. I can't count the number of times I watched "Princess Bride" with my teenage children. Words from the script like "inconceivable," "as you wish," and "mauweeege" remain permanently etched in the archives of my mind. The closing scene is like many other teary-eyed storybook endings where the handsome young prince sweeps the young maiden onto the back of his white stallion as the two fade out into the setting sun to live "happily ever after."

Have you ever dreamed of your own fairy tale marriage? Perhaps you are a young lady waiting for your own Prince Charming to come charging into your life, or maybe you're a young man longing for your Cinderella to show up before the stroke of midnight. Do you find yourself from time to time daydreaming about living "happily ever after" in a state of marital bliss?

Many young people view courtship through the fantasy lens of a storybook and wonder why they do not live "happily ever after." As followers of Christ, we must continually align our thoughts and imaginations with the reality in which we live. As glamorous as it might appear, your life is not being lived out on the colorful pages of a storybook. Your life reflects a world that God describes in His book of truth. Its opening chapter does not begin with "Once upon a time...." Instead, it begins with, "In the beginning God...."

The Bible tells the story of the first marriage between a man and a woman—Adam and Eve—how they loved each other, and how they lived happily together for a short time in the Garden of Eden. We read how this happiness was shattered through their willful rebellion against God's one rule not to eat of the Tree of the Knowledge of Good and Evil. As God promised, a curse of sin and death fell upon this first couple and was passed down to their descendants (Romans 5:12). From that moment, conflict replaced happiness in marriage as wives would desire to rule over their husbands and husbands would actively lord over their wives (Genesis 3:16).

Today, we live in a fallen world, not a fairy tale world—a world that is broken, twisted and scarred by sin, a world where couples, absent the grace of God, do not live "happily ever after." Before we explore God's narrow pathway of blessing in marriage, we should stop and take a

Book Signing

Friday, October 2nd
2-4 p.m.

Abednego Book Shoppe

Finding the Right One
In Light of the Beatitudes

A must-read for every Christian parent and single person seeking God's will for a happy marriage.

DONALD THOMAS

WHAT'S
INSIDE

FINDING THE RIGHT ONE
IN LIGHT *of the* BEATITUDES

sobering look at the pains and heartache that can follow those who refuse to pursue marriage God's way.

Heartache of Divorce

Those who hold to the theory of "biological evolution" often attempt to explain our ever-changing culture through its twin sister, "cultural evolution" This evolutionary mindset leaves no room for marriage to be understood as a non-changing God-ordained union between one man and one woman for life. To reflect the world's philosophies, it must be a dynamic, ever-changing expression of our twenty-first century, post-modern values. President Barack Obama recently explained his own radical transition from opposing same sex marriage to one of full endorsement as the product of his own "evolving" thoughts on marriage.

The world around us appears to be in a moral free fall. God's hand of restraining grace seems to have been pulled back from the hearts of sinners. On this downward spiral can be heard cries for marriage to evolve. No longer is marriage a permanent lifelong union. Gender roles within marriage have been redefined by the acceptance of a radical feminist agenda. Hearts filled with murder have given rise to the legalized abortion of millions of unborn children. Sexual perversion has resulted in the legalization of same sex marriages in most states.

As Christians, we must reject the world's evolving view of marriage and stand firm on the unchanging foundation of God's Word. We must affirm our conviction that marriage was ordained by God, as one of His creation ordinances, for His glory and the good of mankind (Genesis 2:24-25). A Christian marriage is a lifelong covenant-union of one man and one woman in Christ for the mutual benefit of each other and the propagation of the human race. Marriage is a joining together by God of two individuals to become one flesh. Jesus described it as a permanent union: "Wherefore they are no more twain, but one flesh. What therefore God hath joined together, let not man put asunder" (Matthew19:6). In Romans 7:3, Paul reminds us that barring God-sanctioned exceptions, the law of marriage is only broken by death.

The dismal truth is that many marriages, which joyfully started out with much promise, were tragically terminated by a painful divorce. Sadly, many of these broken marriages were between professing Christians who vowed before God that they would remain married "till death do us part." George Barna's polling of American families reveals that, of those who have exchanged wedding vows, 33% have experienced at least one divorce.[1] The divorce rate for those professing to be "born again" Christians bears little difference with that of the unbelieving world.

These statistics are more than numbers. They represent lives, lives that have been wounded and scarred by divorce. Having counseled and prayed with many broken families, I can sadly say that there are few pains in this life greater than the agony of divorce. As distressing as

---

[1] https://www.barna.org/barna-update/article/15-familykids/42-new-marriage-and-divorce-statistics-released#.VCnnevldVOI (updated 2009).

it is to grieve over the death of a spouse, it pales alongside the pain of divorce. Jesus declared that two shall become one flesh. There is no painless way to rip off a piece of your own flesh. You must rip apart skin and muscle before you begin to break bones. In a marriage, it cannot be done without ripping apart and breaking a person's heart.

This extreme pain of separation by divorce is not unlike the severing of a limb. Aron Ralston, an accomplished rock climber, found himself alone and trapped for five days by an 800 pound boulder, pinning his arm to a Utah canyon wall. His only route of escape was to amputate his own arm. His only tool was a dull, broken-down Leatherman knife which he used to first cut through his skin down to his muscles, arteries, and a finally through a bundle of spaghetti-like nerves. In a National Geographic interview, Aron was asked, "But did it hurt?" To which he answered, "When I amputated my arm, I felt every bit of it. It hurt to break the bone, and it certainly hurt to cut the nerve. But cutting the muscle was not as bad. Overall, it was a hundred times worse than any pain I've felt before. It re-calibrated what I understood pain to be."[2] As grueling an experience as that must have been, now multiply the pain of cutting off your arm by 10,000 and you will begin to feel the pain of a spouse cutting themselves free from their own flesh with the rusty knife of divorce.

As both an attorney and pastor, I have counseled and prayed with fathers who have heard it decreed by an earthly judge that their role of father had come to an end.

[2]http://www.news.nationalgeographic.com/news/2004/08/0830_040830_aronralston. html (Updated October 28, 2010).

As the gavel came down, they no longer had physical custody of their children. They were relegated to the new role of "weekend dad."

I've prayed with single moms who had been abandoned by their husbands, leaving them overwhelmed to care and provide for their children. They feel the weariness of working full-time to pay the bills. They know the feelings of loneliness, having been rejected by their closest friend, helper and lover. They often bear the guilt of wondering what they had done to drive their spouse away.

Perhaps the greatest pain of all is that inflicted on the children who must grow up in single parent households. This means children without dads to bring them up in the nurture and admonition of the Lord or the loving tender care of a mom.

My parents divorced when I was two years old. I was raised by a loving, single working mom who sacrificially cared for me during my early years. As much as my mother did to be both father and mother she was unable to remove the heartache of growing up without a father who cared. I can still remember Friday after Friday staring through the chain-link fence outside my fourth grade classroom, wondering if this would be the day that my father would come and visit me.

Do you see why this decision of who you marry is so important? Don't be impulsive. Avoid the danger of emotionally rushing into a relationship. A hasty decision can lead to a life of heartache and pain not only for yourself, but also for your children. Instead, be wise, seek godly counsel, and search carefully for a spiritual heart.

This is God's pathway to a blessed marriage that brings glory to Him.

Heartache of Marriage

Even marriages that are never terminated by divorce can be filled with a lifetime of heartache. Marriage alone cannot bring you happiness. Today, there are many couples who are married and miserable! Neither is there any husband nor wife that can make you happy in this life. True happiness can only come from a peace with God through trusting in His Son and delighting in His purposes for your life. God blesses a marriage with happiness as two believers grow in the grace of God and love each other with a Christ-like love.

However, whenever sin and "self" take reign in either of a couple's hearts, there you will find a marriage filled with heartache. Scripture warns of such misery in verses like: "It is better to dwell in the corner of the housetop, than with a brawling woman and in a wide house" (Proverbs 25:24). "Every wise woman buildeth her house: but plucketh it down with her hands " (Proverbs 14:1). "Likewise, ye husbands, dwell with them according to knowledge, giving honour unto the wife, as unto the weaker vessel, and as being heirs together of the grace of life; that your prayers be not hindered" (1 Peter 3:7).

My grandfather and grandmother remained married all of their lives, but whenever I would visit them as a small child, it was a two-step process. I would first stop in and visit my grandma in her house, and then I would exit out the back door and visit my grandpa who lived in a small travel trailer in the backyard. There, he spent most of his last days smoking his cigars as he glided back and forth on a big canvas swing. Grandpa was only allowed to come in to use the restroom off the back porch. It never occurred to me as a small child that something was wrong. I thought it was normal for grandparents to live apart. I learned later that their lives were filled with painful conflict, severe enough that they lived independently on the same property. In much the same way, many married couples coexist under the same roof, but their hearts are filled with bitterness and anger toward each other.

There are even deeper heartfelt pains that come from a believer who is unequally yoked with an unbeliever. You can live under the same roof without bowing to the same God. One of our family's dearest friends is a godly saint who is married to an unbelieving husband. She chose to ignore her father's oversight as well as the counsel of godly friends and married a very handsome, yet unsaved, young man.

Her prayers and testimony are a continuous reminder to the unmarried of our church of the pain and heartache that can come from being married to a non-Christian. God graced their marriage with nine children and her grandchildren now number in the fifties. She loves her husband, but has lived out half a century of marriage in loneliness and heartache. Her husband never let the children attend church with her. She prays alone, reads the Scriptures alone, and has navigated through life without an earthly spiritual head.

But her heart is plagued by an even greater torment. One day she came into my office with tears in her eyes, lamenting that unless God should graciously intervene, there will be more than fifty of her own flesh and blood who will spend eternity in hell as a result of her one act of disobedience.

A painful, unhappy marriage can fall within the wedding vow of "for better or for worse." Subject to a change of heart, it can extend, by another vow of "to death do us part," bringing a lifetime of heartache. For many, this lifetime of suffering can be averted by prayerfully looking on the heart and asking God what's inside *before* you marry.

Heartache of Children

A child's heartache is not limited to the divorce of his parents. The person you marry may well affect the lives of your children and grandchildren, not only in this life, but for all eternity.

Listen to one of the most sobering texts in all of Scripture: "who keeps lovingkindness for thousands, who forgives iniquity, transgression and sin; yet He will by no means leave *the guilty* unpunished, visiting the iniquity of fathers on the children and on the grandchildren to the third and fourth generations." (Exodus 34:7 NASB). God is not teaching that a genetically induced sin curse is passed on to the children where they suffer both the sinful acts as well as the punishments of their parents. The only genetic curse that exists is found in our relationship to our *first* father,

Adam. As a result of the Fall, we were born sinners by nature and face death as judgment from God (Romans 5:18). We all stand guilty before God for our personal sins, not those of our parents (Ezekiel 18:20).

But there is a warning in the verse: the patterns of a father's sins are often repeated in the lives of his children. The obvious result is that the children, as well as the father, now stand guilty before God for a particular sin. The good news is that, by God's grace, any child can repent of the sins he mirrors of his parents and can turn to Christ for forgiveness.

Often the sins that I lament over most in my children's lives are the very sins I struggled with in my own walk with Christ. I witnessed a graphic example of this verse early in my ministry. Each Lord's Day, I would go with a close friend to our county jail in northern California to preach the Gospel. We would come back during the week and meet with the men, one on one. One weekday evening, we met with a man we knew as Mr. White. The second man we counseled that night also introduced himself as Mr. White. Our third and fourth scheduled appointments that evening were with two other inmates whose names were (I think you guessed it), "Mr. White." With our curiosity pricked, we couldn't help but ask the last man if any or all of the four "Whites" were related. We learned that the older Mr. White was the father of the three younger Whites. Here's the surprise ending: each of these four men was in jail for a separate unrelated drug crime. The sins of the father had passed down to the next generation.

What's Inside

Both your sins as well as those of the person you marry might well pass down to the next generation. If you marry a man who fails to spiritually lead his own family, you will likely raise a son who grows up failing to lead his own family. A stubborn and argumentative wife might raise stubborn and argumentative daughters. Wife abusers often raise the next generation of wife abusers. Drunks may give rise to the next generation of drunks. This pattern is repeated over and over again.

There are also painful, and at times deadly, natural consequences that flow from sinful parents to their offspring. One day a mother came to my office in tears because she had no food or diapers for her children. She told me that she came to the church because she did not know where else to turn. Her husband was unemployed and spent his days at home playing video games. We found him to be a lazy man who refused all opportunities to work at the expense of his family's wellbeing.

The spread of HIV/AIDS in Africa is epidemic. There are many causes suggested for this out of control infection rate including unprotected sexual relations outside of marriage, contaminated needles used by drug addicts, and the large percentage of women who have turned to prostitution in response to the deep poverty. By 2015 it is estimated that 25 million children worldwide will be orphaned by AIDS.[3] A sad reminder of how the sins of parents can pass down generationally.

Most tragic of all, the selection of the person you marry could well have eternal consequences on the souls of

[3] http://www.aidsorphan.net/hiv-and-aids (updated 2013).

your children. I unwaveringly affirm the sovereignty of God in the salvation of souls. However, it is equally true that God frequently chooses to use ordinary means to bring about His purposes. At times, He reaches down with His hand of grace and plucks sinners out of the worst dysfunctional families. I am eternally grateful that He chose to do so in my own life. However, God often chooses to use the ordinary means of godly parents, who are seeking first His kingdom and righteousness, to save the souls of their children. Not only do they bring the Gospel message into their children's ears, but they consistently live out the Gospel before their eyes.

Sadly, the converse is also often true. In homes where there is nothing more than a veneer of Christianity, the children are quick to spot a hypocritical faith. These are families where the children flee from Christ. Absent intervening grace, they will eternally follow the unbelieving steps of their parents. Leonard Ravenhill clearly illustrates this contrast between children of godly parents and children of sinful parents in his book, *America is Too Young to Die*:

> *Max Jukes, [an] atheist, lived a godless life. He married an ungodly [woman], and from this union there were 310 who died as paupers, 150 were criminals, 7 were murderers, 100 were drunkards, and more than half of the women were prostitutes. His 540 descendants cost the State one and a quarter million dollars [before inflation].*
>
> *Then there is a record of a great man of God, Jonathan Edwards. He lived at the same time as*

Max Jukes, but he married a godly [woman]. An investigation was made of 1,394 known descendants of Jonathan Edwards, of which 13 became college presidents, 65 college professors, 3 United States Senators, 30 judges, 100 lawyers, 60 physicians, 75 army and navy officers, 100 preachers and missionaries, 60 authors of prominence, one Vice-President of the United States, 80 public officials in other capacities, 295 college graduates, among whom were governors of states and ministers to foreign countries. Jonathan Edwards' descendants did not cost the state a penny.[4]

Are you beginning to see why this question of who you marry is so important? The pathway to marriage takes you through a fractured, fallen world rather than the enchanted land of the fairy tale. It's a path that leads you to the juncture of a spiritual fork in the road. Every dad, as well as every single person, must decide whether they are going to pursue marriage God's way or their own. The most blessed path is the one where your way and God's way are one. This road leads to happiness and blessing while the other is likely the way of heartache and pain.

As you prayerfully consider your path, remember God's warning: "There is a way which seemeth right unto a man, but the end thereof *are* the ways of death" (Proverbs 14:12). With God's help, I want to shine the light of His Word brightly down this pathway of blessing that it might

---

[4] Leonard Ravenhill, *America Is Too Young to Die* (Minneapolis, Minnesota: Bethany Fellowship, 1979), 112.

seem so glorious, so compelling that you can't help but want to enter in. Where will your first step take you? You will notice that at the intersection of these two paths there is one to greet you in the right way that leads to blessing and life.

In the next chapter, you might be surprised to discover that God has not left you alone. Rather, He has brought someone very dear to your heart to guide you through this important process of discovering the right one.

Chapter 2

Paternal Protection

So then he that giveth her in marriage doeth well...

- 1 Corinthians 7:38

One film that each of our daughters watched just prior to her wedding was the classic comedy, "Father of the Bride." The opening scene shows Annie, now twenty-two and having just returned from Rome, excitedly sharing her explosive good news with her father, George Banks:

> **Annie**: *Okay! I met somebody in Rome. Um, he's an American. Uh, he's from L.A., actually. And um, his name's Bryan MacKenzie. And he's this completely wonderful, wonderful, amazing man, and...well, we started seeing each other, a lot.. and, um...we fell in love. Ha! Ha! It actually happened! And, uh, we've decided to get married...which means that I'm engaged! Ha! I'm engaged! I'm getting married! Ha!*[5]

What's missing from this picture? George Banks is not only caught off guard, but he never even met this Bryan MacKenzie. He is like many dads today, completely removed from the courtship of their daughters. Perhaps the thought of a parent, especially a father, taking the parental oversight of a daughter's courtship has an antiquated

---

[5] Frances Goodrich and Albert Hackett, *Father of the Bride* Script, directed by Charles Shyer, (Touchstone Pictures, 1991).

Victorian ring to many people. The modern parent—and even many professing Christian parents—has totally abdicated this God-given role.

Instead, many Christian families today let their sons and daughters follow the unbiblical practice often referred to as "recreational dating." Typically, this works something like this—it's Friday night! Date night! A young lady gets a text, "W2HO" (Want to hang out?). A cute guy drives by, honks his horn, and off they go on their "date." For many, dating begins in the early teens without any oversight, and the opportunities that can lead to sexual sin are many. Recreational dating often leads to fornication. Fast forward to the point where the daughter finds herself emotionally head over heels. From there it is not a big jump to marriage. Recreational dating is a system that compromises purity, lacks discernment, discourages commitment, and can often be a recipe for a broken marriage.

The pursuit of God's will in marriage begins with parental oversight. There has been a recent resurgence in Christian circles in what has been popularly referred to as "biblical courtship." It is beyond the scope of this book to plumb the depths of courtship. There are several good resources I would recommend every parent and single person read and discuss together.[6]

The term "biblical courtship" is a little misleading. It has a ring of rigid monolithic steps that must be followed in every pursuit of marriage. In fact, many of these steps

---

[6] Douglas Wilson, *Her Hand in Marriage: Biblical Courtship in the Modern World* (Moscow, Idaho: Canon Press, 1997); Joshua Harris, *Boy Meets Girl: Say Hello to Courtship* (Sisters, Oregon: Multnomah Press, 2006).

are more pragmatic application of God's Word than firm biblical steps. At the heart of biblical courtship is parental oversight. More precisely, *paternal* oversight. God has given the father authority to guide his daughter as she pursues God's will in marriage. Although this book focuses primarily on a father's role in his daughter's courtship, a father's authority also extends to the son as long as he lives at home. The father has been given authority over his daughter to protect her purity, discern the spiritual heart of the young suitor, and Lord willing, grant permission and give the young man his daughter's hand in marriage.[7]

This role of the father is nothing new. It's not even Victorian. It's biblical! For those of you who look to God's Word as your sole source of authority in life, you will find this to be God's pattern taught throughout the Bible! Take up your Bible and join me in a quick overview of the father's role leading up to marriage.

Henry Smith, the sixteenth century puritan preacher known as "silver-tongued Smith," first takes us to Genesis 2:18 as a reminder that this paternal authority finds its origin with the first married couple in the Garden of Eden:

> *In the first institution of marriage, when there was no father to give consent, then our Heavenly Father gave His consent: God supplied the place of the father, and brought His daughter unto her husband, and ever since, the father after the same manner, hath offered his daughter unto the*

---

[7] Genesis 24:3-14; Numbers 30:3-5; Deuteronomy 22:13-21; Psalm 78:63.

husband...[8]

As we turn to the book of Exodus we discover the father's role in marriage predates the Mosaic Law. "And if a man entices a maid that is not betrothed, and lie with her, he shall surely endow her to be his wife. If her father utterly refuse to give her unto him, he shall pay money according to the dowry of virgins" (Exodus 22:16-17).

Here we have a man who sexually seduces a young lady, causing her to lose her virginity. The couple desires to marry. The young man informs the father of his intent and brings a dowry. Notice that there is an important condition in verse 17, *If her father utterly refuse to give her unto him....* God has given the father the authority to accept or refuse the giving of his daughter in marriage.

After the giving of the Mosaic law, God brought the Jews into the land to possess it. He promised to deliver them from their enemies and gave them this command: "Neither shalt thou make marriages with them; thy daughter thou shalt not give unto his son, nor his daughter shalt thou take unto thy son" (Deuteronomy 7:3).

Next. we read in Nehemiah how this *giving* and *taking of* sons and daughters was reaffirmed by God's people who covenanted together, "And that we would not give our daughters unto the people of the land, nor take their daughters for our sons" (Nehemiah 10:30).

An objector might stop at this point in protest, "That was then and this is now! What about our twenty-first

---

[8] Henry Smith, Sermon: *"A Preparative to Marriage* (1591)*"* from the Works of Henry Smith, ed. T. Fuller, 2 vols. (Edinburgh: J. Nichol, 1866), Vol. 1, 43-47.

century culture? We no longer have arranged marriages and expensive dowries." This raises the question of whether a twenty-first century Christian father still has oversight of his daughter in matters of marriage.

Let's keep reading! As we turn in our Bibles to the New Testament our Lord reaffirms this teaching in Matthew 24:38 and even extends it to His second coming and the resurrection of the dead in Matthew 22:29-30. Mark Chanski concludes, "Fatherly *giving in marriage* held sway from creation to Noah and should be practiced on earth until the Lord's return and final resurrection of the dead."[9]

In 1 Corinthians 7, Paul divides women into two categories: *virgins* and *wives* (1 Corinthians 7:34). The virgin was the non-married daughter. If she is not divorced or widowed, Paul continues to reason that she remain under her living father's authority. He adds that it is the father that gives his virgin in marriage (v. 38).[10] This biblical truth has passed down today through ceremonial tradition. Most weddings today open with the father walking his daughter down the aisle. When the pastor asks, "Who gives this woman to be married to this man?" the father replies, "I do." However, for the Christian father, this should be more than mere symbolism. The giving away of a daughter should carry with it an affirmation that he has faithfully adhered to the biblical mandate to oversee his daughter's

---

[9] Mark Chanski, *Manly Dominion [in a passive-purple-four-ball world],* (Merrick, NY: Calvary Press Publishing, 2004), 227.
[10] The ESV and NIV have translated this passage to refer to men who are betrothed to virgins rather than fathers of virgins (KJV, NKJV, NASB). Please read the exposition of this passage in Appendix 2.

courtship. By saying, "I do," he gives his whole-hearted approval and affirms before God and the gathered witnesses that he believes this couple will be equally yoked.

In his commentary on 1 Corinthians, John Calvin rightly concludes:

> *Now this passage serves to establish the authority of parents, which ought to be held sacred, as having its origin in the common rights of nature. Now if in other actions of inferior moment no liberty is allowed to children, without the authority of their parents, much less is it reasonable that they should have liberty given them in the contracting of marriage. And that has been carefully enacted by civil law, but more especially by the law of God. ....Let us know, therefore, that in disposing of children in marriage, the authority of parents is of first-rate importance, provided they do not tyrannically abuse it, as even the civil laws restrict it.* [11]

This raises the question about the adult young lady who no longer lives at home. Is she still under her father's authority when it comes to courtship? The Scriptures do not directly speak of this intermediary category of single women. As we have seen, Paul divides ladies into only two categories: married and unmarried. We read of Lydia, who was living independently of her parents (Acts 16:15).

---

[11] John Calvin, *The First Epistle of Paul the Apostle to the Corinthians*, Calvin's Commentaries (Grand Rapids, MI: Baker Book House, 1981), 267-268.

However, we do not know if Lydia was widowed, never married, or whether her parents were still living.

In biblical times, if a woman was married and her husband passed away, it seems clear that she was no longer under her father's headship and therefore free to marry. In 1 Corinthians 7:39, Paul writes, "The wife is bound by the law as long as her husband liveth; but if her husband be dead, she is at liberty to be married to whom she will; only in the Lord." Even then, it would be both wise and honoring for a widowed daughter to seek the counsel and blessing of her living father.

There seems to be a tendency for our theological understanding to conform to our downwardly spiraling culture. We saw this when the radical feminism of the 1960s became mainstream and had a transformative effect on the church. Many denominations, as well as independent churches, who historically held to the Bible teaching that church office bearers are gender specific, suddenly changed their theology and abandoned their historical understanding of church polity. We see the same shift currently taking place with the ordination of homosexuals in certain church denominations along with the sanctioning of same sex marriage.

Why do I mention this? Because there is currently a similar shift taking place in the teaching regarding a father's role in courtship. There has been a long historical understanding that Paul in 1 Corinthians 7 was giving fathers the mandate to guide his daughter's heart through the emotional waters of courtship. The common teaching often preached today is that Paul was not speaking of fathers and daughters, but rather fathers and the young men who pursue their daughters. This leaves the Christian daughter to proceed toward marriage independent of any paternal guidance. To show you how prevalent this teaching is today, I have added an appendix wherein is an evaluation of an extensive survey I took of pastors from many denominational backgrounds on this very subject. If you are one who normally skips over appendices, I recommend reading it anyway. You might be surprised by my findings.

Paul gives a concluding warning to fathers not to act maliciously against the best interest of their daughter. In other words, with headship comes responsibility.

A loving father, who seeks the purity and blessing for his daughter, will prayerfully evaluate the heart of any interested young man. If he finds him falling short biblically, he has the God-given authority to say "no" to the young man. Dads, giving your daughter's hand in marriage is more than walking down the aisle of the church; it encompasses the authority to give your approval. Young single ladies, this requires you to trust your father as he pursues God's will on your behalf. You are witnessing your father's love in action. Remember, to trust in God is to trust the one that He has graciously placed in authority over you, your father.

Why is this parental oversight so important? It is the God-given means by which a father can discern the heart and intentions of the person desiring to court his daughter. Without spiritual oversight, a young lady is tempted to judge a young man by his outward appearance rather than on his heart. This protects single ladies from being swept away by a man with bursting biceps and wavy blond hair who makes her heart soar, but clouds her ability to discern the absence of spiritual life.

Several years ago, a young man wanted to date one of my daughters. I asked him if he would meet me the next day at a local coffee shop. I knew my daughter was smitten by this young cowboy. He shared with me a short testimony of his faith in Christ. I asked him what he wanted to do with his life. I was shocked by his quick reply, "I want to be a country singer!"

"Oh really," I replied, trying to keep a serious face. "How do you plan to do that?" He gave me his five year plan that began with playing in local bars until he could make it big in Nashville. I brought our conversation to a quick halt by informing him that he would have to pursue his dream without my daughter.

Dads, ask the hard questions of those who are pursing your children. Listen carefully to their testimonies. Inquire about their walk with the Lord of their pastors and other spiritual leaders who know them. Pray to God for wisdom.

I remember another occasion; one of my daughters told a young man who attended the same out-of-town college and wanted to date her that he had to talk first to her dad. He flew into town for three days with the objective of winning my approval. He seemed very likeable. He gave me all the right answers to the questions I asked. However, as we came to the last day of his visit, I had the unsettled feeling that I still didn't know his heart. I prayed that night and asked God, "How can I know this young man's heart in one day?" I remembered the words of our Lord, "But those things which proceed out of the mouth come forth from the heart; and they defile the man" (Matthew 15:18). It suddenly struck me! His words are connected to his heart! I changed my strategy. Instead of asking questions, I would just listen to his words.

The next day I told him to hop in the car; we were going to take a day trip to Yellowstone. My itinerary purposely allotted for a lot of windshield time. I asked a few open-ended questions, but mainly I just listened! There were long awkward spans of silence at first, but on the way home, he began to speak nonstop. He spoke very critically of his theology classes. He didn't know why anyone would want to know theology. I began to hear a heart that was opposed to growing in grace. Then I heard the words of a young man whose passion was clearly for the things of this world. He then told me that he had made a profession of faith as a young boy, but followed this up with a confession that he didn't believe that there was any spiritual fruit in his life. I offered up an exclamatory prayer of thanksgiving for God's clear answer to my prayer.

What if you are unmarried and have an unbelieving father or a father who is disengaged in your pursuit of a spouse from God? It is always wise to go to your earthly father and seek advice. If you do not have a dad who will step up to the plate and help you discern God's will, then seek out other counsel. The important point is, don't go solo in such an important decision. Go to the elders of your church whose ministry it is to shepherd your soul. Perhaps you have brothers who are spiritually mature and wise. Go with a willingness to follow their wise counsel. This will help protect you from making a foolish or emotional decision which might bring lifelong, painful consequences.

We read how Esau left the safety of the Old Testament custom of the arranged marriage. Apparently, without parental oversight or counsel, he chose a Hittite woman as a wife. This sad choice became a grief to Isaac and Rebekah (Genesis 26:34-35).

A more recent reminder comes to us from the marriage of John Wesley to Molly Vazeille. Biographers have described it as "one of the greatest blunders he ever made" and "a preposterous union." The marriage was a train wreck from the beginning. What went wrong? John suffered a great loss when his engagement to Grace Murray failed, and he had vowed to seek his brother Charles' counsel before marrying in the future. But less than three years later, he proceeded alone and hastily announced that he would marry Molly Vazeille. It was a marriage marked by jealousy, strife, and later separation. John Hampson of Manchester "once entered a room unannounced to find Molly dragging her husband across the floor by his hair."[12] What made this an unhappy marriage? Certainly Molly's heart was not right. However, much of their heartaches lay at the feet of John's hasty refusal to consult his brother Charles for marriage advice as he had earlier vowed.

How does parental oversight work its way out in modern courtship? If a young single man is introduced to a young lady with whom he would like to pursue God's will

---

[12] John Charles Pollock, *John Wesley* (London, England: Hodder and Stoughton, 1989), 238.

in marriage, he should first seek the counsel and direction of his own parents. Dads, it is now your duty to take this request seriously and search out the heart of the young lady before giving your approval. Subject to his father's approval, the young man should then go to the young lady's father and request permission to begin "courting" his daughter. Once again, Dad, this is an awesome responsibility given by God. It takes grace to discern the heart and intentions of a young man. It requires your time, prayers, counsel, and heavenly wisdom to know his heart. The daughter's father should exercise due diligence to best know the heart and intentions of the suitor. This will take time. If her dad gives the green light to proceed, he should then set the parameters of the relationship to protect the purity of the couple as they seek together the will of God.

Young people, are you willing to trust God to work His will out through your father? Remember, your father loves you and wants nothing less than your happiness and God's glory! A young man who refuses to come under the counsel of his parents gives great insight into how he will lead as a husband. The "my way or the highway" attitude will weaken the fabric of the home. The same is true with a young lady. If a single lady will not come under the authority of the headship of her father, it reflects a heart attitude that will not submit to the headship of her husband. Seventeenth century historian, Thomas Fuller, gives us these wise words: "If you would have a good wife, marry one who has been a good daughter." What should dads and single people be looking for in the heart of the one who has come courting?

Chapter 3

Marry a Believer

Be ye not unequally yoked
together with unbelievers...

- 2 Corinthians 6:14a

The young couple joyfully announced, "We're getting hitched!" Translation: "We're getting married!" Little did they know that they were using imagery right out of the Bible where Paul warns, "Be ye not unequally yoked together with unbelievers: for what fellowship hath righteousness with unrighteousness? And what communion hath light with darkness?" (2 Corinthians 6:14). Marriage is the *hitching* together of two lives to walk as one.

The picture in 2 Corinthians 6:14 is one that utilizes farming tools of first century Palestine. The yoke was a wooden piece that would fit over the necks of a pair of oxen. Often two oxen were yoked together with a wooden crossbeam to pull a primitive plow behind them. The Law of Moses forbade plowing with an ox and a donkey yoked together (Deuteronomy 22:10).

I asked one of the men in our church who grew up on a Wyoming homestead and is a collector of horse drawn farm machinery why this is so important. He explained that an ox and a donkey don't walk together. They have different cadences and walk at different rates of speed. One is stronger and the other weaker. The stronger pulls on the head of the weaker, twisting it around. Rather than working together, they war against each other until finally, tired of fighting, the plowing comes to a standstill. What a picture of an unequally yoked marriage!

Christians are to *hitch* together with Christians. Believers are to marry "only in the Lord" (1 Corinthians 7:39). It's not an option for the child of God to marry an unbeliever. You might be thinking, "As long as we love one another, what difference does it make if we are both Christians or not? Won't our love for each other overcome that hurdle?" Paul answers those questions with five rhetorical questions of his own: "For what partnership has righteousness with lawlessness? Or what fellowship has light with darkness? What accord has Christ with Belial? Or what portion does a believer share with an unbeliever? What agreement has the temple of God with idols? For we are the temple of the living God" (2 Corinthians 6:14b-16a).

To marry an unbeliever is to marry your spiritual enemy. As long as you are unequally yoked, you can never spiritually become one flesh. You will be yoked together with someone of a different heart, different priorities, affections, and convictions. As you walk through life together, you will be like that ox and donkey, warring against each other until finally your marriage comes to a standstill. You will be unable to cultivate a biblical family life; your marriage will be filled with the weeds of heartache.

In chapter 1, I introduced you to a dear friend who has been married for fifty-plus years to an unbeliever.

Whenever a young person in our church is tempted to pursue an unbeliever I encourage them to go speak to her. She has experienced firsthand the pains and struggles of being unequally yoked in marriage. She tells of her struggles and the sadness of walking alone in the faith. She laments the pain of not being able to share her joy in Christ with the ones with whom she is most intimate. She describes the heartache felt each Lord's Day when leaving her husband and nine children behind and driving to church alone. And oh, how she would love to open her home to the church with a heart of hospitality; but the years have been filled with frustration and, at times, conflict. Outside of Christ, no agreement can be found on marital roles or the nurture, admonition, and evangelization of the children. Finally, there is the anguish of knowing that the man she loves as well as all of her children remain eternally lost unless God should powerfully intervene with His saving grace.

As difficult as such a marriage is, it could be much worse. Her husband could be heavy-handed and abusive. Her family could be stained by impurity. However, this dear saint is married to a man with much common grace. He lives an outwardly moral life and gives her freedom to personally pursue her faith in Christ. Often this is not the case.

To marry a person who is a non-believer is to marry a person who is an enemy of God! The unsaved individual's heart is in love with sin and opposed to holiness. The compromising power of the world will be given free rein to pound on your family daily. It will be seen in worldly entertainment, the movies watched, the games played, the language spoken, the priorities set, and the company kept. A materialistic pursuit of the things of this world will replace the pursuit of the kingdom of righteousness. You will forfeit the delight of being loved by a spouse with a sacrificial, unconditional, Christ-like love.

The greatest danger of all is that your unbelieving spouse might lead you away from Christ into idolatry. The one you love might be the very means that leads your heart into apostasy. The downward path to idolatry is a slippery slope. The first step begins with a heart that desires to become unequally yoked. J. C. Ryle gives this short, pithy definition of idolatry: "I say, then, that idolatry is a worship in which the honor due to God in Trinity and to Him only is given to some of His creatures or to some invention of His creatures."[13]

Once you replace Christ with an unbelieving spouse as the object of your honor and affection, you do so to the dishonoring of Christ. Your spouse becomes that first slippery step which, if left unrepentant, will lead you deeper into a life of idolatry and the ultimate loss of your soul. King Solomon did not marry just one unbeliever; Scripture tells us that he loved and married many unbelieving women who worshipped pagan gods. God warned him, "For surely they will turn away your heart after their gods" (1 Kings 11:2). But rather than heeding the Word of God, he went on to take 700 wives and 300 concubines! As we flash forward, we read of the tragic end of his life: "For it came to pass, when Solomon was old,

---

[13] J.C. Ryle, *Idolatry* (Pensacola, Florida: Chapel Library, Free Grace Broadcaster, 2004), 2.

that his wives turned away his heart after other gods: and his heart was not perfect with the Lord his God, as *was* the heart of David his father" (1 Kings 11:4).

This raises a practical question for dads and all who are unmarried: What does it mean to be *equally* yoked? Putting it in the positive, as it relates to marriage, it's a command to be equally yoked in salvation. Christians are to marry Christians. That means that the person you court is to be one who will first of all have a credible testimony of faith in Jesus Christ (Romans 10:9). He or she should be able to personally verbalize the essential elements of the Gospel. It's not enough to say, "I'm a Christian," "I was raised in the church," "I walked down the aisle and prayed the sinner's prayer when I was six years old," "I had a life-changing experience at a summer youth camp!", or "I turned over a new leaf for Jesus and am trying hard to please God." Without the prompting of your leading questions, a true convert should be able to verbalize God's work of grace in his or her heart.

First, you should hear words of repentance (Luke 13:3). Listen carefully for personal expressions of sorrow for sin and a willingness to turn far from it. Spurgeon warned, "You must be divorced from your sin, or you cannot be married to Christ."[14]

Second, you should hear words that express the wonder of grace. These are words seasoned with humility that exclude all works of self-merit and exalt a God who has done all to save their souls. The forgiven sinner cries

---

[14] Charles Spurgeon, *All of Grace* (New York, NY: Cosimo, reprint 1886), 76.

out, "It's God who saved me! I didn't deserve to have my sins forgiven. What a gift!"

Third, there should be an understanding and expression of what some call "the great exchange." Listen for words that speak of the substitutionary atonement of Christ. This part of the testimony does not have to be couched in theological terminology, but there should be a basic understanding that one's sins were exchanged for Christ's righteousness. After reading, "For he hath made him to be sin for us, who knew no sin; that we might be made the righteousness of God in him" (2 Corinthians 5:21), you might ask, "How does this verse speak to your life?"

Fourth, a testimony should joyfully proclaim salvation through faith in Christ alone (Ephesians 2:8)! Is he or she trusting in anyone or anything for salvation other than the completed cross-work of Jesus alone?

Finally, there should be some verbal acknowledgement that Jesus Christ is Lord (Romans 10:9). Do you hear a heart passionately beating after a life of obedience?

Inquire about baptism. Baptism is our Lord's first command to every new convert. It is fashionable today to take the name "Christian" and bypass publicly identifying with Him through the waters of baptism. The Scriptures closely connect baptism with faith without making it a prerequisite for salvation (Mark 16:16). F. F. Bruce rightly concludes, "Faith in Christ and baptism were, indeed, not so much two distinct experiences as parts of one whole."[15] Spurgeon sees it as a real test of a person's profession of faith:

> *Oftentimes, I believe that this little matter of believers' baptism is the test of the sincerity of our profession of love to Him. It would have been all the same, it may be, if the Lord Jesus Christ had said, "Pick up six stones off the ground and carry them in your pocket and you shall be saved." Somebody would have said, "That stone-picking is a non-essential." It becomes essential as soon as Christ commands it! It is in this way that Baptism, if not essential to your salvation, is essential to your obedience to Christ. If you have become His disciple, you are bound to obey all your Master's commands—"Whatever He says unto you, do it."[16]*

This credible testimony of faith may not fully express itself in one conversation. It might require several meetings. All are not astute in expressing their experiences. A little prodding and questioning may be required on your part. A person's own profession of faith in Jesus Christ might not be seasoned with biblical terminology, but if there is true salvation, a believer can't help but publicly proclaim it!

I must add a brief word of warning here about the new convert. What about the person who is a relatively new believer? Perhaps he or she grew up in an unbelieving

---

[15] F. F. Bruce, *The Letter of Paul to the Romans: An Introduction and Commentary* (Grand Rapids, Mich.: Wm. Eerdmans 1985), 129.

[16] C.H. Spurgeon, "Baptism Essential to Obedience," from *The Metropolitan Tabernacle Pulpit,* Vol.39 (London: Passmore & Alabaster, 1893), 601.

home and during the last semester of college had an encounter with Christ through a campus ministry. What about the person who suddenly professes faith in Christ after being attracted to a person who is already a Christian? In either case, the *older* believer is often delighted and rushes into a courtship thinking the matter of being equally yoked has been settled. It well could be that the grace of God has wonderfully brought this one to the Savior, but it is also possible that he or she has only a spurious faith. With the anemic gospel that is popular on many college campuses, it could be that the young college student had nothing more than an intellectual or emotional experience that fell short of trusting in Christ alone. There is the additional danger of a person jumping through the hoop of faith with the sole motivation of pursuing a relationship with a believer.

This raises a problem: How do you know a person's true motives? Prior to attending our church, a young Christian lady had been attending a college ministry at another church. She met a handsome police officer who was also attending the same college group. One day, he asked her out on a date. Knowing that he was not a believer, she faithfully declined his invitation. A few weeks later, he proclaimed his dramatic conversion. They dated. They became engaged. They married. He soon departed from the faith. Five years later, their marriage tragically ended in divorce. Sadly, this scenario has been repeated over and over again.

It is good to wait before you court a recent convert. Wait and see how the person's profession of faith sails through a few of life's storms. For this very reason, I recently counseled a young lady to wait on the Lord rather than rushing into a courtship. Wisdom would dictate that enough time should pass for spiritual fruit to be manifested from a changed life (Matthew 3:8). Remember, in the parable of the sower, only the seed that fell on good soil bore fruit, indicating true salvation. All who have been graced with a new heart and trust in Christ alone for salvation will bear the fruit of a changed life. Beware of courting the stony-ground hearer who joyfully confesses Jesus for a while, but withers and dies spiritually when the scorching trials of life come (Matthew 13:5-6)!

There will be greater happiness in your marriage where there is greater unity. The heart of being equally yoked should extend beyond salvation. It is important for a couple to be as much as possible of "one mind." Paul exhorts fellow believers to "complete my joy by being of the same mind, having the same love, being in full accord and of one mind" (Philippians 2:2).

An important area of oneness should be in the doctrines of the Christian faith. A popular mantra of our day states, "Doctrine divides, but love unites!" In other words, as long as we love one another, it doesn't matter what we each believe. The Bible confronts this reasoning by telling us that love and truth are inseparable. Paul describes a believer's attitude this way: "But speaking the truth [doctrine] in love" (Ephesians 4:15a). Spiritual truths are not dead, ethereal concepts reserved for ivory tower theologians; doctrine is glorious spiritual truth that translates into practice.

Does this mean that a couple should be in complete

agreement on every point of doctrine? If you are to be equally yoked in truth there must be agreement on the essential truths of the faith. There can be no unity when there are opposing views of such doctrines as the Trinity, Christ, the Gospel, and the Word of God.

More than likely, there will never be complete agreement on every small point of doctrine. A premillennialist can have a happy marriage with an amillennialist. In fact, some of these minor differences can actually have an iron sharpening iron impact on the married couple.

Apparently the learned theologian John Calvin did not make perfect doctrinal unity an element in his own courtship and marriage. The Reformers and the Anabaptist (re-baptizer) movement stood in theological opposition to each other. At odds were their views on such teachings as baptism, the Lord's Supper, perfectionism, and the source of revelation. After a failed courtship at the age of thirty-one, Calvin was tempted to give up on marriage altogether. He wrote, "I have still not found a wife, and I doubt that I'll look for one anymore." To everyone's great surprise, Calvin was married two months later to Idelette de Bure, an Anabaptist widow with two children of her own.[17]

Since Idelette was a member of Calvin's church she must have come to embrace much of the Reformed faith. It is believed that she continued to hold on to some minor doctrinal differences and she might have had an influence

---

[17] John Witte, Jr. and Robert M. Kingdom, *Sex, Marriage, and Family in John Calvin's Geneva, Vol.* 1, *"Courtship, Engagement, and Marriage"* (Grand Rapids: Wm. Eerdmans, 2005), 99.

in shaping Calvin's view of strict church discipline. In spite of any minor theological differences, the couple was graced with nine happy years of marriage that was cut short by Idelette's early death. Seek to be equally yoked in the essential areas of the Christian life. The period of courtship is a good time to explore these areas.

On what doctrines should there be unity? Each couple must work this out according to their own convictions. There are many doctrines that have the potential of affecting the harmony and spiritual life of the family, such as baptism, the doctrines of grace, and the person and work of the Holy Spirit.

On the surface, differences on baptism might seem insignificant. However, the practice and mode of baptism become particularly important at the birth of the first child. It is a matter that should be explored before you say, "I do." Freely ask questions like, "Should a baby be baptized? Should babies be sprinkled as a sign and seal of the covenant of grace (paedobaptist view), or should baptism be reserved until the child professes faith in Christ (credobaptist view)? How will our respective views affect which church our family will attend?"

This was the question facing my Baptist son and the young Congregational lady he met in college. My son traveled to New England to seek her father's permission to begin courting her. Before her father said, "Yes," he wisely gave the couple a book in support of the paedobaptist position. He asked them to prayerfully read and discuss the book together, looking up all the supporting Scriptures. I later called my son and asked him how his study on baptism was going? He said, "Dad, before I read the book, I was a Baptist because you raised me a Baptist, but now I am a Baptist by conviction!" The young lady's father was happy with the way the two had agreed to work out their differences practically, and he warmly gave my son permission to court his daughter.

A second important area of harmony should be found in the doctrine of salvation. It is wise to discuss whether the beliefs of the couple are anchored in the doctrines of sovereign grace or the "freewill" of man. Although to some this might sound trivial, the foundational doctrine of God's sovereignty is one of those doctrines that has historically divided believers. This was a doctrine that brought division to my own family. I loved my parents and made it my pursuit to honor them. Yet, our deeply divided convictions over the sovereignty of God resulted in them never coming to hear me preach during the first twenty-five years of my ministry or witness the baptism of any of their seven grandchildren.

Like all doctrines, this one has its own practical out-workings. I have come to believe that the sovereignty of God is one of those "continental divide" doctrines that affect a person's beliefs and practices in many other areas, including worship, spiritual growth, and approaches to evangelism.

Third, seek unity in the doctrine of the person and work of the Holy Spirit. Is there agreement on the gifts of the Spirit? Your answer will have a big bearing on where you attend church as well as how you worship God.

Finally, there are many other doctrines worth

exploring during a courtship, if for no other reason than to know the depth of the other person's scriptural understanding. Let me encourage you to make your courtship conversations spiritual. It might be fun to discuss compatibility in music styles, favorite foods, and movies, but what a blessing it is to explore your unity and understanding of such matters as end times (eschatology), worship, the role of women in the church, the centrality of preaching, children's ministries and programs. You might be thinking, "Do these things really matter?" Absolutely! They matter enough to the Lord to teach these things in His Word.

I recently witnessed how seemingly minor beliefs have the potential to divide a family. A couple moved to our town and began attending our church. Both attended at first, but soon the husband came alone. We later learned that the wife did not share her husband's views on church polity (government), and that she refused to attend any church that held solely to male leadership. She had found her own church that held to the modern egalitarian view of leadership. After attending separate churches for over a year, the man sadly shared with us that, for the sake of peace in his family, he would begin attending the other church with his wife.

In addition to doctrinal unity, a couple should explore their oneness in the essential areas of practical Christian living. Here are a few questions you can ask each other:

- *How many children make a full quiver?*
- *What are the biblical roles of husband and wife?*

- *Should wives work outside the home?*
- *What does the Bible teach about childrearing?*
- *What are your convictions about personal finances, giving, stewardship and indebtedness?*

What are some other questions you would like to add to your own list?

Dads, it is God's calling for you to faithfully discern the salvation of the person seeking to court your son or daughter. This is not an easy duty to discharge. It requires you to pick up your magnifying glass, put on your Sherlock Holmes hat, and do some spiritual detective work. Ask questions. Listen to testimonies. Don't hesitate to seek the counsel of your elders. Interview others who might know the person first hand. Ask to be friends on their Facebook. Social media is a rich mine of information for discerning a person's heart. Above all, pray for wisdom for God to help you know the person's heart. He promises to answer your prayers.

Many young people are tempted to cut spiritual corners at this point, perhaps out of fear of becoming an "old maid" or a prince without a princess. Maybe you find yourself reasoning, "No one is perfect! Isn't it better to be married to an unbeliever than never to be married at all? After all, even in the fairytale the maiden kisses a frog before it turns into a dashing prince. Won't God do the same thing for me? Maybe the unbeliever will be saved by my witness!" The issue is not what God can or can't do; it is what God will have you do. He will work out His good in your life as you seek first His kingdom and righteousness.

A dear single friend of mine had a passion to be

married. As long as I knew her, she had prayed that God would bring her a godly husband. She faithfully continued to trust God for His provision until she turned forty. Her greatest fear, as one of my Scottish pastor friends recently told me, was being "put up on the shelf." One day, during a moment of weakness, the tempter came knocking. A tall, handsome, blond man seemed to suddenly appear out of nowhere. She later discovered that he was an active member of a cult, but by this time, she was already swept off of her feet emotionally. She kissed her frog! She married her frog, and he remains a frog to this day! The life of joy she so longed for suddenly became a life of sorrow.

Our Lord's command does not end with the command to not be unequally yoked. Paul continues, "Wherefore come out from among them, and be ye separate, saith the Lord, and touch not the unclean *thing*; and I will receive you, And will be a father unto you, and ye shall be my sons and daughters, saith the Lord Almighty" (2 Corinthians 6:17-18).

God's marriage plan is for a young prince to marry a young princess, not a frog! A prince is a son of the King! A princess is a daughter of the King! May God grace you in marriage with a child of the King!

When a person outwardly confesses faith in Christ, how can you know their inward heart? Do you take them at their word?

Chapter 4

Marry the Merry!

Blessed are...

- Matthew 5:3

All of the arrangements had been hastily made for our elopement. I had purchased a used wedding band from the back room of a local jeweler and the beautiful church building just on the edge of the University of Nebraska campus had been reserved. Mary and I, after her last class on Friday, would quickly cut across campus to exchange our vows—two unbelieving college students with no true biblical understanding of marriage. We said our "I do's" and headed off to Valentino's Pizza with a few friends. I don't share this with you as a pattern to follow. If anything, it is a testimony of the abounding grace of God to a couple of clueless, undeserving rebels.

In reflection, I've wondered why it was so important for the two of us to be married by a pastor in a church building. I have to confess that it seems a little hypocritical. After all, I rejected every other plan and purpose of Christ for my life, so why did we both want a Christian service in a church building? There were times when I thought it was nothing more than tradition. Had all of those Hollywood romantic movies had their way with me? But I have come to believe that it was more superstition than tradition. As strange as it might sound, I truly felt that our marriage would be more "blessed" if it were performed by a real minister in a real church building with a real steeple. I had a doubting fear that perhaps our marriage would not "take" if Mary and I ran off to a garish Las Vegas wedding chapel with the service conducted by an Elvis look-a-like. After all, isn't a "blessed" marriage everyone's dream? I wish marital happiness was as simple as being married in a church building. If that were the case, divorce court would become a thing of the past.

In truth though, the pathway to a happy marriage begins before the wedding, even before the engagement. It begins by courting a person with whom you are equally yoked in faith and practice. This raises a practical question: How can you be sure the person you desire to court has a true, passionate faith in Jesus Christ? As we saw in the last chapter, you must listen for a credible testimony of faith. But it mustn't stop there.

Many young singles are satisfied with a shallow profession of faith alone. Others might go a little further, not only listening to someone's testimony, but also taking notice of their outward religious conduct. Perhaps they are further convinced by their regular attendance at church, Bible study, or general knowledge of the Bible and conclude, "Wow! What a committed Christian!" But we must remember that not all church attenders are true worshipers of God. Neither are all who tote name-embossed, leather Bibles lovers of God and His Word. As commendable as these things might be, if you stop there, you are making the potentially fatal error of looking on the outside rather than examining the heart.

I sat across the desk from a broken man. Tears

streamed down his face, staining the divorce papers which were clinched in his hands. Not only was he threatened with the breakup of his marriage, but also the loss of custody and visitation of his two precious children. His marriage had a storybook beginning. He and his wife grew up together in the same Baptist church. They attended the same Christian school and youth group. After a short engagement, they joyfully marched down the church aisle while family and friends cheered their new life together.

Unfortunately, the person they kissed before God and the congregation was someone other than the person they thought they knew. Both were attracted by the costume of outer religion. They failed to discern each other's inner heart. Jesus might have described them as two beautiful "whitewashed tombs" exchanging their wedding rings and vows. Neither of them realized that their new spouse was "full of dead men's bones" (Matthew 23:27). It wasn't long after the honeymoon that their masks of hypocrisy were removed. The dream marriage, which started off so happily, quickly turned into a nightmare. The wife began to reveal the heart of an adulteress. She secretly solicited other male companionship over the Internet. Eventually, she abandoned her family for a "virtual" man who lived in India. The husband took off his own religious mask and responded in kind with his own salvos of sin. Just shy of their fifth anniversary, divorce papers were filed.

This couple dropped completely off my spiritual radar until one day, several years after their divorce, the young man burst into my office and blurted, "I've got some good news for you; I'm doing better and I've gone back to church!"

I think he was hoping to hear congratulatory words of encouragement. But instead, I responded, "Not church! Why would you want to go back to church? That's what contributed to your divorce in the first place!"

Confused, he asked, "What do you mean? I thought you would be happy that I'm going back to church."

I began to explain. "You and your former wife attended church together all of your lives. You were involved in church activities. You were both steeped in religion, which only masked two wicked and deceitful hearts. Your church attendance did not result in a changed heart." I went on to encourage him to continue going to church as an ordinary means of grace, but I reminded him that his greatest need was not more religion, but true conversion that only God could bring through the new birth. I pleaded with him to repent of his sins and flee to Christ. I told Him I would be praying that God might grace Him with a new heart.

Our Lord never tells us that we can know someone is a Christian by his testimony or church attendance (Matthew 7:20). The work of God in the life of every true convert produces spiritual fruit unto holiness (John 15:5; Matthew 13:23; Galatians 5:22-24). Authentic Christians do not wear the camouflage of this world. They stand out brilliantly, reflecting the light of Christ. Jesus reminds us, " Ye shall know them by their fruits. Do men gather grapes of thorns, or figs of thistles? Even so every good tree bringeth forth good fruit; but a corrupt tree bringeth forth evil fruit. A good tree cannot bring forth evil fruit, neither *can* a corrupt tree bring forth good fruit. Every tree that bringeth not forth good fruit is hewn down, and cast into the fire. Wherefore by their fruits ye shall know them" (Matthew 7:16-20).

How can you know a person's heart? God cautions that the heart is wicked and deceitful. This keeps us from fully knowing our own heart, let alone that of another (Jeremiah 17:9). Yet God has given us the stethoscope of His Word to detect a spiritual heartbeat. The natural heart is cold, granite-hard, and spiritually dead. When God wonderfully saves a sinner, He replaces that heart with a heart of flesh that beats with spiritual life (Ezekiel 36:26). From this new heart, God wonderfully produces life that bears Christ-exalting spiritual fruit (John 15:4).

There are several lists of spiritual fruit found in the New Testament. In Galatians 5, Paul contrasts the deeds of the flesh with the nine-fold fruit of the Spirit (Galatians 5:22-24). John, in his first epistle, describes the essential heart changes that mark every true Christian so that they might have full assurance of eternal life (1 John 5:13). Our Lord introduced His Sermon on the Mount with eight happiness-producing attitudes that mark every citizen of His heavenly kingdom. You will find each of these character qualities present in varying degrees in the life of every true believer. Look and listen carefully for each of these Beatitudes during your courtship as you prayerfully try to discern the other person's heart.

The opening verse of Matthew 5 transports us to a grassy mountain area. This mountain is certainly not like the majestic Rockies that dwarf us here in Wyoming. More than likely, it was a grassy hillside on the north shore of the

Sea of Galilee. This mount formed a natural amphitheater where the words of Christ resonated in the ears of the multitude that followed Him. He led them up along the slope where He would sit down with His disciples in the recognized posture of a teacher. The apostle Matthew now brings us to the feet of the preacher, Jesus Christ, who describes eight characteristics that you will find present in every true Christian. Martyn Lloyd-Jones concludes:

> *First, all Christians are to be like this. Read the Beatitudes, and there you have a description of what every Christian is meant to be. It is not merely the description of some exceptional Christians. Our Lord does not say here that He is going to paint a picture of what certain outstanding characteristics are going to be and can be in the world. It is His description of every single Christian.*[18]

The first word from our Lord's lips is "Blessed" (v. 3) from the Greek word *makarios* which simply means "happy." The true Christian is a happy Christian. This is not a whimsical giddiness that is found in external pleasures. It might be best understood as bliss or an inward sense of contentment that comes from an inward change of heart. It is a state of inward blessing and joy that every Christian experiences as God increasingly produces the fullness of His Son in their lives. It is a God-given, soul-satisfying happiness that can only come from knowing and growing in Christ. It is nothing like the fleeting happiness of this world, which is sparked by the stimulation of the

---

[18] D. Martyn Lloyd-Jones, *Studies in the Sermon on the Mount,* (Grand Rapids, Mich.: Wm. Eerdmans, 1976), 25.

flesh. Many are pursuing this temporal happiness that is found in sin, but only for a season (Hebrews 11:25). The book of Proverbs warns that the one who loves pleasure shall be a poor man (Proverbs 21:17). The last days are marked by men who are lovers of pleasure rather than lovers of God (2 Timothy 3:4).

The reason so many people miss true happiness in this life is that they are looking for it in all the wrong places. It is a sad paradox that their sinful hearts stubbornly reject the only One who can produce this state of bliss. The melodramatic covers of the supermarket tabloids are reminders that true soul-satisfying happiness will never be found in thick portfolios, fleeting outward beauty, jet-setting getaways, heart-thumping entertainment, stately mansions, or even fifteen minutes of fame. True happiness will be found only in Christ.

This is the very reason why many couples never discover true marital happiness. They wrongly pursue it in external stimulants that bring only unsatisfying, temporary jolts of pleasure. There is the husband who fantasizes that his marriage will be a happy one when his wife loses fifty pounds. Then there are the couples who both slavishly work, driven by their passion for happiness that will be found in a new home.

I counseled with a young couple whose marriage was fractured by conflict. I looked each of them in the eye and asked what it would take for their marriage to be truly happy. I wasn't prepared for the husband's quick response, "A million dollars!" Somehow he reasoned that if he was suddenly blessed with a million dollars, his joy-robbing burden of indebtedness would be replaced with prosperity and a happy marriage. I pointed him to these words of one of the wisest of all men: "He that loveth silver shall not be satisfied with silver; nor he that loveth abundance with increase: this *is* also vanity" (Ecclesiastes 5:10). Whatever temporary jolt of joy these worldly pleasures might bring, they are at best fleeting and fail to satisfy your soul with lasting happiness.

I saw a graphic picture of this mindset several years ago in the grandfather of TV reality shows entitled "Who Wants to Marry a Multi-Millionaire?" The plot was predictable. Fifty beautiful women, one from each state, flirtingly competed to be the future wife of a multi-millionaire bachelor. Following their superficial interactions, the bachelor selected a blonde beauty from California as the apple of his eye and married her on the spot. The new bride sported a 3-carat diamond wedding ring and received $100,000 in additional prizes. They set sail for a honeymoon in Barbados and their life of living "happily ever after." Surely this mix of fame, fortune, and beauty would be the perfect recipe for marital bliss. Not so quick! The couple's troubles began immediately after tying the knot. They spent their luxury cruise in separate cabins. When the new bride returned home, she immediately filed for an annulment.

Here is the key to a happy marriage: No person or thing, other than Almighty God, can bring lasting happiness to your life! Any other source of happiness will be vain and fleeting at best. People change and often deceive us. How many spouses have been tempted to exchange their mate for another whose youth or beauty brings them a quick fix of happiness? Marital happiness for many couples is conditioned upon their financial state. No wonder fighting over finances is one of the leading causes of divorce. Paul reminds us, "For the love of money is the root of all evil:" [including divorce] (1 Timothy 6:10). The Puritan, Thomas Watson, poetically paints this picture of the shallow, fleeting happiness that this world offers:

> *Worldly delights are winged. They may be compared to a flock of birds in the garden, that stay a little while, but when you come near to them they take their flight and are gone. So 'riches make themselves wings; they fly away as an eagle toward heaven' (Proverbs 23:5). They are like a meteor that blazes, but spends and annihilates. They are like a castle made of snow, lying under the torrid beams of the sun.*[19]

True happiness is more than a temporal state of being. It is the state of being a child of the King. It is the person who, by God's grace, bears the marks of all eight of our Lord's Beatitudes. Jesus declares that person "blessed," "happy," and "contented." It is the blessing of God that brings you to fulfill the chief end for which you were created, "to glorify God and enjoy Him forever!"[20]

A God-blessed marriage is a happy marriage. True marital happiness begins when a man and woman, who have both been saved by the blood of Jesus Christ, enter into a lifelong covenant to carry out God's purpose in

---

[19] Thomas Watson, *The Beatitudes* (Edinburgh: Banner of Truth Trust, 1971), 27.
[20] First question, Westminster Shorter Catechism.

marriage. God promises each of them His happiness as their lives increasingly embody the eight Christ-like characteristics found in the Beatitudes. During every marriage ceremony I perform, I remind the couple of this truth with these words:

Happiness is not found in marriage alone. It will be found as you both welcome the will of God, the Word of God, and the person of God into your new home as both Companion and Guide. You will find that two lives drawn close to Christ will also be drawn close together.

How can I know if the person I am courting is truly a happy person who bears the marks of the Beatitudes?

Chapter 5

Marry the Poor

Blessed are the poor in spirit...
- Matthew 5:3

Many couples who publicly vow to take each other as husband and wife, "for better or for worse, for richer, or poorer" inwardly think, "But richer would be much better." Conventional wisdom tells us that marital happiness is found in marrying a rich person. Girls are often told by their mothers, "It's just as easy to love a rich man as a poor man." Perhaps you have heard: "No romance without finance." However, God's way to true happiness defies conventional wisdom. It is not found by the multitudes on the broad expressway that leads to destruction. It is only found by those few who, by God's grace, enter through the small gate onto that less traveled narrow way that leads to life. In this first Beatitude, our Lord reminds us that true happiness is not found in wealth. Instead, He declares, "Blessed [happy] are the poor in spirit" (Matthew 5:3).

Before we discover what it means to be "poor in spirit," let's take a step back from the Beatitudes and observe how our Lord weaves them together. I don't believe that our Lord randomly listed them. As we are going to see, each Beatitude is dependent on the one before it. Think of the Beatitudes like a train. All the cars must be present, and yet poverty of spirit, like the engine, leads the way with the caboose of persecution tagging along at the end. This is important because it means that all of the Beatitudes will be present in varying degrees in the life of every Christian. Where there is one grace, you will find all. Although all of the Beatitudes are present, all are not perfectly present. Some might be barely sprouting while others might be seen as bountiful bouquets of God's grace. Remember, every believer is growing in the grace of God.

Why does our Lord begin with poverty of spirit? It is this heartfelt attitude on which all the other Beatitudes are built. It is the fertile soil from which God grows rich, spiritual fruit.

What does our Lord mean by "poor in spirit"? The original Greek word for poor, *ptochos,* is much stronger than our English equivalent. Poverty in America allows for three meals a day, a roof overhead, a car, a flat screen television, a personal computer and access to the Internet. In 2010, there were 46.2 million Americans labeled as *poor.*[21] What is *poor* today? According to the Census Bureau, poverty may be defined as a family of four whose annual income is $22,541 or less.[22] I can remember those days when I was a *poor* college student working part time for Gerber Baby Foods. Thanks to the company discount, I was able to add strained peaches to my normal diet of *Top Ramen* and peanut butter sandwiches. The American definition of poverty is the world's definition of wealth.

Poor in the biblical sense is better translated *destitute, penniless,* or *totally bankrupt.* I learned firsthand

---

[21] Timothy J. Essenburg, Lindsey K. Hanson, ed., *The New Faces of American Poverty* (Santa Barbara: ABC-CLIO, 2014), 173.

[22] *Poverty Definition* U.S. Census Bureau. Accessed: 2003-12-27.

our Lord's meaning of poverty on a mission trip to Hermosillo, Mexico. We had to drive through the city dump to bring needed provisions to several families living on the other side of town. It was a hot summer day. Our windows were rolled up to stem the stench of garbage and keep flies from biting. Out of the trash heap, we heard a faint voice calling us. To our surprise a tiny head poked up out of the newspapers and plastic bottles. Our hearts ached with pity for this young boy, no more than seven years old, whose only shelter was a cardboard box and only food that which he could scavenge from the daily garbage.

A person who is "poor in spirit" is a person without resources to bring to God, unable to earn God's favor, and one who is completely left to His mercy. This is that awakening grace of God that brings a person to suddenly realize that he is spiritually bankrupt. Individuals are brought to see that all of their acts of righteousness, which were once thought so valuable, are worth nothing more than "filthy rags."

Our Lord is painting the picture of a sinner who is brought by the grace of God to see his spiritual poverty. This is the person who looks up and sees the huge self-amassed sin debt. Guilty sinners stand like unrighteous beggars, naked before God, because they know that there is nothing they can do to remove that mound of iniquity. All of their acts of religion are worthless. No baptism can wash away the stench of their sins. God responds with contempt to all of their zealous acts of religious rigmarole. It's regarding this kind of poverty that Augustus Toplady penned in his hymn, "Rock of Ages":

What's Inside

Nothing in my hand I bring,
Simply to the cross I cling;
Naked, come to thee for dress;
Helpless, look to thee for grace;
Foul, I to the Fountain fly;
Wash me, Savior, or I die.

See why our Lord begins with "poor in spirit"? Only then will sinners humbly cry out to God for mercy. Only when they realize that they have no righteousness of their own will they cry out for Christ's righteousness! Marry the person who realizes that he or she is spiritually worth zero!

One of the best New Testament illustrations of poverty of spirit can be found in the parable of the Pharisee and the publican in Luke 18:9-14. What a contrast between the hypocritical religion of the Pharisee and the poverty of spirit of the publican! The Pharisee was puffed up with pride and self-glory. The publican was broken, humble, and poor in spirit.

Full of self-sufficiency, the Pharisee prayed, "God, I thank thee, that I am not as other men are, extortioners, unjust, adulterers, or even as this publican. I fast twice in the week, I give tithes of all that I possess" (Luke 18:11-12).

While afar off there was another man, a sinful tax collector, who, beating on his chest, cried out to God with a heart that was poor in spirit, "God be merciful to me a sinner" (Luke 18:13). Jesus tells us that only the publican went away justified.

Five Marks of Spiritual Poverty

Happy is the person who marries downward. Happy is the one who marries a person who is not rich in himself, but poor in spirit before God. This raises a practical question. How can you know if a person's heart is marked by the riches of self-righteousness or true spiritual bankruptcy? Dads and single Christians, here are five helpful marks of those graced with poverty of spirit:

#1 – Sees Himself as a Helpless Sinner

Before you enter into a courtship, be sure you listen carefully to the person's personal testimony. Are you hearing words that express spiritual poverty? You should hear an acknowledgement of God's mercy and grace rather than personal merit. The spiritually poor sing, "Nothing in my hand I bring, simply to the cross I cling." These are the ones that recognize that they have a zero balance in their heavenly account.

A person who is not poor is spirit is a person rich in himself. Beware of those who speak proudly of their religious accomplishments or are quick to dismiss their sins as no big deal. As you listen carefully to conversations, the rich in spirit will speak little of repentance, will rationalize their sins, and are quick to blame others for their failures. The poor in spirit recognize that they are what they are by the grace of God alone.

#2 – Trusts in the Cross of Christ Alone

When God brings sinners to see themselves as spiritually bankrupt, unable to do anything to rescue themselves from the wrath of God, they flee to the only One who can save them, the Lord Jesus Christ. Unwilling to trust in themselves, they now trust in Christ's sacrificial death on the Cross as full payment for their sins. They flee to Christ, surrendering on His terms. Thomas Watson graphically describes this heart of surrender:

> *A castle that has long been besieged and is ready to be taken will deliver up on any terms to save their lives. He whose heart has been a garrison for the devil, and has held out long in opposition against Christ, when once God has brought him to poverty of spirit, and he sees himself damned without Christ, let God propound what articles he will, he will readily subscribe to them, 'Lord, what wilt thou have me to do' (Acts 9:6). He that is poor in spirit will do anything that he may have Christ. He will behead his beloved sin. He will, with Peter, cast himself upon the water to come to Christ.*[23]

This is important as you listen for a credible testimony of faith in Jesus Christ. You might hear how a person asked Jesus into his heart at the age of six. This common profession fails to express words of repentance and faith alone in the person and work of Christ. You shouldn't hear any merit coming from their religious activities or good works. Are you hearing "Thy" or "I"? The self-righteous will be heard saying, "I walked down the

---

[23] Watson, *The Beatitudes*, 47.

aisle," "I attend a college Bible study," "I go to church," "I, I, I." Instead, the spiritually poor will speak much of "Thy" (Christ's) work on the Cross. Christ's blood will be precious. They will often be heard echoing the words of Paul, "This *is* a faithful saying, and worthy of all acceptation, that Christ Jesus came into the world to save sinners; of whom I am chief" (1 Timothy 1:15). Just because a person's testimony lacks clear expressions of spiritual poverty does not necessarily mean that the individual is not trusting in Christ. The giving of a clear testimony of faith has not been taught or modeled to many young Christians today. You should not be afraid to dig a little deeper. Ask some probing questions about sin, the work of Christ, and their true hope for salvation.

A young man came asking if he could court one of my daughters. At our first meeting, the conversation turned quickly to his testimony. I said, "Tell me how you became a Christian." He told me about his life of sin and how he repented of his sins and was trying to live the Christian life. He seemed to have a clear understanding of sin and his need to repent. But there appeared to be something missing. Suddenly it struck me that there was no mention of his faith in the sacrificial death of Christ on the Cross.

I rephrased my question several times. Each time he gave the same testimony. Probing a little deeper I posed the question this way, "If your neighbor saw you attending church on Sunday and asked, 'Are you a Christian?' How would you answer?"

He was quick to reply, "I would tell him, 'Yes, I am a Christian.'"

I then asked if his neighbor were to say, "Please tell me how I too can become a Christian," how would he answer him?

He paused and confessed, "I'm not sure. I guess I would point him to the Bible and tell him, 'The answer can be found somewhere in here.'"

I gently proceeded to share with him the reasons why I could not give my permission for him to court my daughter. At the top of my list was my concern that they might be unequally yoked. I stressed with him the importance of a credible testimony of salvation by grace alone through faith alone in Christ alone. What was missing from his testimony was Christ's work on the Cross for his sins. I went on to explain to him that repenting and trying to lead a good life falls short of trusting in Christ alone. The Lord used this encounter to help him see that he must first be poor in spirit before He will ever see his need for Christ. On a positive note, several months later, God turned on the light of understanding, and the man was brought to realize that he had nothing to bring to God. All along he had been trusting in himself rather than Jesus. God wonderfully saved him, and he shared a glorious testimony of Christ's salvation before his church family and friends as he was baptized.

#3 – Continually Asks for God's Mercy and Gives Thanks

A person who is spiritually rich with self-righteousness will have little for which to be thankful. All who are spiritually bankrupt realize, "Every good gift and every perfect gift is from above, and cometh down from the Father of lights, with whom is no variableness, neither shadow of turning" (James 1:17). Remember, the tongue is the mouthpiece of the heart. Those rich in self-righteousness are self-sufficient and neither ask for God's mercies nor give thanks to Him.

Beggars, on the other hand, drop to their knees and continually plead to God for His mercy. Is the person you are considering to court a praying person? Is prayer an integral part of your relationship? Do you hear humble petitions to God to supply daily needs? Listen carefully for prayers of gratitude. Is this a person who is thankful to God and others for their acts of kindness? Listen carefully during family conversations. Do you hear boasting or gratitude?

#4 – Delights in Service

There are no jobs too small or demeaning for the poor in spirit. They are grateful that they can be counted with the least of the servants in the Kingdom of God. You will find them joyfully heeding the command of Jesus to wash one another's feet. Think what your family life would be like if you were not married to a servant. Self-centered spouses rob their families of both life and joy.

Many husbands and fathers are AWOL from their families because their own agendas trump the needs of their wives and children. You will find them to be game-playing, couch potatoes, or conjoined with the guys, but that is not what a husband or father was meant to be. God has called the husband to lovingly lead his wife.

What does this leadership look like? It bears the image of Jesus Christ as both Servant and Lord. Servanthood demands that husbands be there for their families. The servant leader puts the needs of his family above His own. The serving husband will arrange his schedule so as to spend time daily in family worship. God has called the man to lovingly protect, provide, and cultivate his family in every way to keep it from going to the weeds.

It will be the delight of the serving wife to sacrificially care for the daily needs of her husband and children. Nothing is too good for her family. She bears the marks of the virtuous woman in Proverbs 31. You won't find her routinely sleeping in, but setting her alarm to prepare a hearty breakfast for her family. She is often up late into the night caring for the needs of her husband and children. She has a heart of compassion for others. She carves out time from her busy schedule to bring gifts to the needy. No wonder her children rise up and bless her while her husband offers his praise (Proverbs 31:28).

I think it wise during the courtship process that occasions for service be introduced into the relationship to offer opportunities to display poverty of spirit. One of my sons courted his wife for four years. She lived several hours away, and the only time they could see each other was on weekends. My daughter-in-law's father was very wise. Every week he had some new project laid out for my son. During those courtship years, my son helped build a cabin, roof a house, cut down and stack firewood, along with other strenuous outside chores. Not only was this girl's dad measuring my son's work ethic, he was looking to see if this was a man with a servant's heart.

A young man was courting the daughter of a couple who are very close to our family. He satisfied the father's initial interrogatives, and the young couple began their pursuit of seeking God's will regarding marriage. The family thought the best way to get to know this young suitor was to include him in many of their family activities. They became concerned when they noticed what appeared to be an absence of a servant's heart. Things quickly came to a head when they included him in a family camping trip. Their minivan was packed tight with camping gear. They arrived at the beach just as the sun began to fall over the Pacific. Dad and the kids scurried to set up the tents and gather firewood before dark set in. Mom unpacked the food and started dinner. Where was our young man? He sat passively by, watching the camp being set up. His lack of help did not go unnoticed. After returning home, the young lady and her dad discussed the importance of a husband having a servant's heart. The rich in spirit demand service while the poor in spirit humbly serve. They both agreed that the young man's lack of service was significant enough that they brought the courtship to a halt.

#5 – Gives Glory to God

Every Christian should be prepared to answer this one important question before entering into a courtship: What is my ultimate purpose in getting married? In other words, why get married? You might be quick to answer,

"To love and enjoy each other for the rest of our lives," or "God willing, to raise a family." These are good reasons for getting married, but both fall short of God's ultimate purpose. God's purpose for marriage is no different than His purpose for all areas of your life. Paul declares, "Whether therefore ye eat, or drink, or whatsoever ye do [including marriage!], do all to the glory of God" (1 Corinthians 10:31). The *Westminster Shorter Catechism* underscores Paul with this reminder, "Man's chief end is to glorify God, and to enjoy Him forever."[24] Jonathan Edwards summed up God's purpose in his life this way: "God's purpose for my life was that I have a passion for God's glory and that I have a passion for my joy in that glory, and that these two are one passion." The rich in spirit find their treasure and delight in themselves and this world. Only the poor in spirit find their greatest joy in Christ and His glory!

Marks of a God-glorifying Life

How do you know if the person you would marry is one who glorifies and enjoys God in every area of his or her life? Do you see an obvious desire to submit to Christ's lordship? Here are four marks of a God-glorifying life. Find out if the person you wish to court:

#1 – Produces Spiritual Fruit

Just prior to the Cross, our Lord gave this mark of

---

[24] Westminster Shorter Catechism, Q. 1.

true discipleship:"Herein is my Father glorified, that ye bear much fruit; so shall ye be my disciples" (John 15:8). Hold the person you would court up to the mirror of Galatians 5:16-25. Do you see a life marked by the works of the flesh or the fruit of the Spirit? In those who are poor in spirit, you will find love, joy, peace, patience, kindness, goodness, faithfulness, gentleness and self-control on display for the glory of God!

#2 – Praises God

The Psalmist pens, "Whoso offereth praise glorifieth me: and to him that ordereth *his* conversation *aright* will I shew the salvation of God" (Psalm 50:23). Is the person a worshiper of God? Is the Lord's Day his delight? You will not find the poor in spirit sleeping in, surfing or playing golf on the Lord's Day. Is there a passion to gather with the people of God on the first day of the week to hear His Word proclaimed and to praise Him in prayer, singing, and the breaking of bread? Be on guard for the person who frequently makes excuses for skipping church. The poor in spirit find their delight in fervently worshipping the greatness of their Lord with God's people.

#3 – Prays According to God's Will

The poor in spirit will be found often on their knees. God tells us that He is glorified as we come asking for all within His will. Jesus promises, "And whatsoever ye shall ask in my name, that will I do, that the Father may be glorified in the Son" (John 14:13). Consider whether the person you are courting is one who wants God's will over his own in every area of life. If so, he will be one that cries out for God's will in the selection of a career, a place to live, guidance in family planning, church membership, and Christian service.

#4 – Proclaims the Gospel

God is most glorified in the Gospel of His Son (1 Timothy 1:11). We glorify God as we proclaim the Good News to sinners who flee to Christ for forgiveness. The more souls that are saved, the more thanksgiving and praise is offered up for the glory of God (2 Corinthians 4:15). The poor in spirit have a burden for lost sinners. Do you hear your intended praying for the souls of unconverted friends and loved ones? Does the object of your affection take delight in sharing a personal testimony with others? Is there evidence of being missions minded? Is there a generous spirit of giving to evangelistic ministry outreaches?

Conclusion: The Dual Blessings

Don't miss the dual promises that God attaches to all who are truly poor in spirit. First, they will be found "blessed" (i.e., happy). This isn't a future heavenly blessing; this is a present tense, here and now blessing. All who are poor in spirit *are* happy! God graces them with a life of joy and blessings now. That means if you are poor in spirit and marry a person who is poor in spirit, two happy people will be joined into one spiritually happy couple.

Secondly, our Lord promises, "Theirs is the

kingdom of heaven" (Matthew 5:3b). What a wonderful paradox! Those whose lives are marked by spiritual poverty will be happy not only now, but they inherit all the riches of citizenship both now and forevermore in the Kingdom of God.

Marry the poor and you will be blessed. What Beatitude follows poverty of spirit?

Chapter 6

Marry the Sad

Blessed are they that mourn...

- Matthew 5:4

Your wedding day is one of the happiest days of your life! It is a day filled with laughter and delight. Family and friends stand united, watching you walk down the aisle and exchange vows. It is a day complete with a reception of warm hugs and kisses. It is a festive day with tasty hors d'oeuvres topped off with a piece of the mile-high wedding cake, a day that slowly fades into a romantic honeymoon.

Every couple expects that their marriage day will be the first day of a lifetime of happiness. Unfortunately, for many, this marriage that began in merriment turns to sadness. Here is an important paradox for you to remember as you consider the person you are to marry:

Marriages that begin with merriment end in tears. Marriages that begin in tears end in merriment.

As we saw in the opening chapter, if your marriage is to be merry, do not become unequally yoked. Marry a Christian. Marry a like-minded, fellow believer. How do you know if a person is a true believer? This is the question that our Lord is answering as we continue our journey through the Beatitudes. In the last chapter, we saw that the foundational attitude of all Christians is poverty of spirit.

Marry a person who sees himself as spiritually bankrupt, one who sees his sin debt with God as so huge that there is nothing he can do to pay it. By the grace of God, he sees himself as spiritually bankrupt and totally empty of any righteousness. He has become a spiritual beggar, crying out for mercy.

God's work of grace does not stop with our awareness of poverty. If it did, we would be left to a life of spiritual dumpster diving, a futile life of scavenging in a hopeless search for that which only God can supply. When God saves a sinner, He first awakens him to his spiritual poverty from which He then produces a heartfelt mourning.

Jesus declares, "Blessed [happy] are they that mourn" (Matthew 5:4). Happy are the sad. That sounds like doublespeak. What does Jesus mean by *mourn*? How does sadness bring happiness? He is not advocating a life of asceticism where religious sojourners search for peace through deprivation of all physical pleasures. We must keep in mind that Jesus is speaking in the spiritual realm, not the physical. In the parallel passage given in Luke 6:25b, our Lord reverses the order: "Woe unto you that laugh now! for ye shall mourn and weep." Do you see the contrast? Those whose lives are marked by frivolity and laughter now will ultimately face eternal weeping, but those who mourn now will be happy and eternally comforted.

The word *mourning* is a strong word in the original. It means much more than a general feeling of sadness. It expresses exceedingly great mourning which includes lamenting or wailing caused by huge tragedy or loss. It is much like the grief experienced at a funeral, anguish so deep that it cannot be contained or concealed. Jesus is speaking of spiritual mourning. Here our Lord speaks of the happiness that comes to those who mourn, lament, and wail over their sins.

Here you must be careful. Not all sorrow for sin yields salvation and blessing. Paul warned the Corinthians to beware of a false sorrow, "For godly sorrow worketh repentance to salvation not to be repented of: but the sorrow of the world worketh death" (2 Corinthians 7:10). Beware of the worldly sorrow that falls short of salvation. This is a sorrow that leads to eternal death!

What is this worldly sorrow for sin? It is a sorrow that falls short of true repentance. This is the sorrow that comes when you feel bad for doing bad. This is the remorse that you feel when you are caught and your sins are exposed. This is the sorrow of the world that drives people to drink, depression, and even suicide. This is the sorrow you hear from the lips of politicians caught up in scandal when they stand before the cameras and confess, "I'm sorry if my conduct offended you in any way." What is missing in the sorrow of this world? A sadness over breaking the law of a Holy God, followed by a willingness to turn from sin by God's grace.

The best portrait of this worldly sorrow might be seen in the face of Judas Iscariot who betrayed Jesus Christ for thirty pieces of silver. As soon as the silver coins dropped into his sweaty hands of betrayal, he felt the sorrow of guilt in his heart. He knew what he had just done was terribly wrong and he felt awful. In Matthew 27, we can see how closely false sorrow can mimic true godly sorrow. When Judas realized that he was condemned, he "repented himself" (v. 3). This is a different word than the one normally translated "repentance" in the New Testament. It means that he felt guilty and remorseful. It falls short of true repentance that humbly seeks God's forgiveness accompanied by the fruit of turning from the sin.

Look how closely Judas' repentance (remorse) mimics true godly repentance. He made a failed attempt to make restitution. In his own way, he tried to make things right by attempting to return the silver to the priests and elders (Matthew 27:3-4). He was heard making a public confession of his transgression before men: "I have sinned in that I have betrayed the innocent blood" (v. 4). Finally, he even threw the ill-gotten gain into the temple coffers (v. 5). His sorrow was not a sorrow unto life, but a sorrow unto death. In graceless despair, rather than fleeing to Christ, Judas went out and hung himself (v. 5). Judas went further than many professing Christians go today in response to their sins, yet he fell short of true repentance.

Marry a person who mourns over his sins with a godly sorrow that leads to true repentance. These are the ones who acknowledge that they have transgressed the law of God and stand broken and guilty before Him. You won't hear from them a general confession, "God, forgive me; I am a sinner," but rather, a repentance of specific sins, "God, please forgive me; I'm an adulterer, or a covetous person."

Here are the marks of godly sorrow. It is mourning

that:

- hates sin
- forsakes sin
- confesses sin to God and those wronged
- trusts in the blood of Christ to cleanse
- quickly seeks to make restitution.

This is not a one-time sorrow. It is not a temporary prick of conscience that takes place before a response to an emotional altar call. Our Lord is speaking in the present tense. Happy are those who continually mourn. As they are convicted of new sins, they mourn and turn from those sins. An ongoing repentance is the pattern of their lives. It is said of British Reformer and martyr, John Bradford, that his personal walk with Christ was of a deep devotional nature. He was in the habit of writing down his faults because he wanted to feel a "chest-beating" regret for sin and groan with true brokenness of heart when he came to private prayer.

There can be no salvation without repentance. Mourning for sin is a mark of grace. James calls sinners to "Draw nigh to God, and he will draw nigh to you. Cleanse your hands, ye sinners; and purify your hearts, ye double minded. Be afflicted, and mourn, and weep: let your laughter be turned to mourning, and your joy to heaviness" (James 4:8-9). Spurgeon correctly reminds us that faith and repentance are two sides of the same coin.

Puritan Thomas Watson warns that the opposite of holy mourning is "hardness of heart" or "a heart of stone" (Ezekiel 36:26). He observes, "A stone heart is not sensible to anything. Lay weight upon it; grind it into powder; it does not feel. So it is with a hard heart."[25] A stone heart of unbelief cannot shed a tear or feel sorrow for sin.

Marry the sad and you will be happy. This raises the question: How can you know if a person is mourning over his sin? You can never know for sure. However, I would encourage you to beware of a person that bears these marks of a hard heart:

1. **A love for sin.** A person who does not mourn over sin is a person who loves sin and desires to continue in it. He might profess faith in Christ and attend church regularly, but if he loves sin, he does not have a heart of repentance. The more you are around a person, the more this will become clear to you. Rather than encourage you in your walk of holiness, he or she will be an instrument of temptation in the enemy's hand.

   - Listen carefully to the way he talks. Remember, the tongue is the heart's spiritual EKG. Listen carefully. What do you hear? If a person talks long enough, he will be unable to mask his true spiritual identity. Lips filled with cursing, off-color jesting, gossip, anger, criticism, and lying could well be joined to a heart that remains rock hard.

   - Watch closely at the way he walks. There are only two pathways: one is broad that leads to destruction and the other is narrow and leads to life (Matthew 7:13-14). Where do his

---

[25] Watson, *The Beatitudes,* 72.

footsteps take him? Do they lead to movies filled with profanity and impurity? Where does he seek out entertainment? How does he treat others? How does he manage his finances? Remember the prodigal son who squandered his inheritance on his sinful passions. A person who is mourning over his sins is a person who hates sin and loves God with all of his heart.

2. **A rationalization of sin.** A person who mourns over his sin is not perfect (1 John 1:8). Our ultimate perfection will come when we see Jesus face to face. Until then, we are growing in grace. However, one who does not sorrow over his sins often discounts, rationalizes, and blame shifts. Remember Adam and Eve's response when they were caught sinning in the Garden of Eden? Adam was quick to blame Eve and indirectly blame God for giving her to him. Eve immediately pointed her finger at the serpent. Is the person courting you quick to shift the blame when he has broken God's law? Do you frequently hear him trivialize or make excuses for his transgressions? The Christian's pathway is a lifelong battle for holiness. The true believer does not make light of the enemy.

3. **A presumptuous relationship with God.** Dry eyes and a hard heart do not stop many today from confessing that they are Christians. The popular "easy-believism" gospel of our day heralds the message to simply believe in Jesus for eternal life. You can have Jesus and your sins! You can enter

heaven without holiness. A trusting in Christ that excludes a turning from sin is nothing more than a presumptive relationship with God. J. C. Ryle correctly connects the necessity of faith and repentance:

> *But I am bold to say that the two graces are never found separate, one from the other. Just as you cannot have the sun without light, or ice without cold, or fire without heat, or water without moisture—you will never find true faith without true repentance, and you will never find true repentance without lively faith. The two things will always go side by side.*[26]

Those with presumptive faith are left with only a hollow profession. That is why you will often hear them speak of their faith in the past tense. They might proudly declare, "I walked down the aisle when I was five years old." They are quick to pawn off the faith of their parents as their own as they tell about their life growing up in a Christian family. Those who are truly mourning over their sins have a living faith in the here and now. They are soldiers engaged in a spiritual war. You might learn much by simply asking, "How is the battle going?"

4. **A life full of frivolity.** The person with a hard heart is a person who views life as a big joke. You might find it difficult to see any evidence of spiritual seriousness. Life is seen aa one big party. Spurgeon

[26] J. C. Ryle, *Old Paths* (Carlisle, PA: Banner of Truth, 1999), 407-408.

observes:

> *There are others who are all froth and
> levity, who profess to be Christians, and yet
> cannot live without the same amusements as
> worldlings. They must be now at this party,
> and then at that. They are never comfortable
> unless they are making jokes and following
> after all the levities and frivolities of the
> world.*[27]

It might just be a symptom of immaturity or it might
mean a heart that does not mourn over sin.

This Beatitude brings with it good news for all who
are repentant and mourn over their sins. Jesus promises that
"they shall be comforted" (Matthew 5:4b). Notice the
order: tears over sin precede comfort. Weep for sin now,
forsake your wicked ways, and then God will comfort you.
This is just the opposite of the way Satan comes to snare
you. The devil always tempts with pleasure first. He
dangles before you the glitter of this life. Beware! God
warns that such frivolity is followed by eternal weeping!

What is the comfort that this mourning brings? First
of all, the person who mourns is really happy! The
bloodstained hands of Jesus come and wipe away their
tears of repentance, and the Holy Spirit exchanges them for
a smile of true happiness and heartfelt contentment. Their
sole joy and delight is now in Jesus Christ. There is no
greater comfort than that which comes from knowing, with
full assurance, that all of your sins are forever forgiven by

---

[27] C. H. Spurgeon, *The Metropolitan Tabernacle Pulpit*, vol. 14 (reprint,
Pasadena, Tex.: Pilgrim, 1979), 97.

His blood!

Where does this comfort come from? Jesus speaks of another Comforter, the Holy Spirit (John 14:16-18). The Holy Spirit indwells with comfort the lives of all who are poor in spirit as He actively supplies joy, admonishment, conviction of sin, strength, courage, gifts, power, and assurance!

I close this chapter with three reasons why it is essential that you marry the sad.

1. **Because there is so little repentance in today's Christianity.** The popular gospel that is commonly preached falls short of sixteen ounces to the pound. "It is a Christianity in which there is undeniably 'something about Christ, and something about grace, and something about faith, and something about repentance, and something about holiness;' but it is not the real thing as it is in the Bible."[28] It is an "easy-believism" gospel without a call to repent or bow to the lordship of Jesus Christ. Why is this so important to courtship? Many young people who grew up in church youth groups and backyard clubs were called to walk down an aisle, pray a prayer, raise their hand, ask Jesus into their heart without a sorrow for sin that produced repentance. That means that there are many young people who are of marriageable age who have never heard the call of repentance. Rather than mourning over their sins, they are the product of the entertainment driven

---

[28] J.C. Ryle, *Holiness, Its Nature, Hindrances, Difficulties, and Roots* (London: James Clarke & Co., 1952), 10.

youth group with all of its levity and frivolity. Jesus warned that unless you repent, you will eternally perish (Luke 13:3).

2. **Because the "sad" are those who nurture and build strong families.** Those who are mourning over their sins are those whose lives are marked by an active continual repentance. To marry a person with a heart of stone is to marry a person who will be blind to his sins and stubbornly refuse to acknowledge his faults. This leads to a life of painful conflict. To marry the sad is to marry a person who, when he does wrong, rushes to Christ for forgiveness and seeks reconciliation. This is the person who is quick to confess when he has wronged you and strives to restore peace. As long as you are both open to repent and forgive, you will be blessed with a marriage marked by harmony.

3. **Because the two blessings of happiness and comfort are the very blessings that bring happiness and comfort to the family.** The only one who will bring happiness and comfort to your marriage will be a spouse who is mourning over his sins. Jesus is careful to speak the pronoun "they" (*autoi*) as emphatic towards those who are continually mourning over their sins. It is they *and they alone* who shall be comforted.

The question we have been asking is, "God, whom shall I marry?" God's answer is, "Marry a person who is trusting in my Son for salvation." How can you know if a person is truly trusting in Christ as His Lord and Savior?

Listen carefully to his testimony. As we have seen, you will find the heart attitudes of a true believer in the Beatitudes. Marry a person who is spiritually bankrupt. That will be a person who is sad. Look! Listen! Pray that God might lead you to a person who mourns over his sins, a person whose face feels the salty brine of repentant tears, whose heart is continually turning from sin to the arms of the saving Lord.

Listen carefully and you might hear a heart that echoes this Fanny Crosby hymn:

Jesus, My All

Lord, at Thy mercy seat, humbly I fall;
Pleading Thy promise sweet, Lord, hear my call;
Now let Thy work begin, oh, make me pure within,
Cleanse me from every sin, Jesus, my all.
Tears of repentant grief, silently fall;
Help Thou my unbelief, hear Thou my call;
Oh, how I pine for Thee! 'Tis all my hope and plea:
Jesus has died for me, Jesus, my all.
Still at Thy mercy seat, Savior, I fall;
Trusting Thy promise sweet, heard is my call;
Faith wings my soul to Thee;
this all my song shall be,
Jesus has died for me, Jesus, my all.[29]

The Beatitudes should awaken you to the reality that God would have you marry a person who is the direct opposite of what the world tells you to look for.

You might even be more surprised at the next Beatitude.

---

[29] Words: Fanny Crosby, 1866. Music: Bethany (Mason), Lowell Mason, 1856.

Chapter 7

Marry the Meek

Blessed are the meek:
for they shall inherit the earth.

\- Matthew 5:6

An old weathered Wyoming cowboy had been helping lead our weekly Bible study at the county jail. This week was different. I noticed that his right hand was wrapped with bandages. Concerned, I asked, "What happened to your hand?"

"Oh, it's okay," he replied. "I was breaking a wild horse today, got my hand caught in the reins, and ripped one of my fingers right off!" What a graphic display of the power of the horse!

We have wild horses here in Wyoming. Just a few miles east of our house are the Pryor Mountains, known for a large herd of wild Mustang horses. Periodically, when our children were growing up, we would take a break from homeschooling, load up the kids in the "mother ship" (family name for our 15 passenger van), and head off to the Pryor Mountains in hopes of getting a glimpse of these Mustangs. Wild horses are amazingly powerful, unpredictable, self-willed, and often dangerous.

Before a wild horse can become profitable, it must first be rounded up and then broken. One of the men in our church breaks and trains horses for a living. He recently described the training as a two-staged process. First, there is the "starting" stage which involves breaking the will of the horse so that it can be ridden and trained further. Then comes the "finishing" stage: the ongoing training of making the horse more and more useful in doing the will of its owner.

What a graphic picture of all of us in our natural state without Christ. We are all spiritually wild by nature. Paul describes us as lawless enemies of God: "Because the carnal mind *is* enmity against God: for it is not subject to the law of God, neither indeed can be" (Romans 8:7). The spiritually wild, in their rebellious self-will, fight against God as well as those whom He brings into their lives. Peter describes the cadence of the spiritually wild as "them that walk after the flesh in the lust of uncleanness, and despise government. Presumptuous *are they*, selfwilled, they are not afraid to speak evil of dignities" (2 Peter 2:10).

The good news is that God's grace changes all of that. God goes out on the range of humanity and draws in self-willed sinners who snort out defiance as they rear up their heads in rebellion. In this fourth Beatitude, Jesus now describes the "starting" stage where our Owner and Master-trainer, by the power of His Spirit, subdues rebellious sinners and graces them with new hearts marked by meekness. Listen to how Jesus announces this good news, "Blessed are the meek: for they shall inherit the earth" (Matthew 5:5).

Our training does not stop at the "starting" stage of new hearts adorned with meekness. There is an ongoing "finishing" stage of sanctification that continues for a lifetime. It is the work of the Holy Spirit, who progressively grows us more and more in Christ-likeness.

Who are you to marry? Marry a fellow Christian. You ask, "How will I know a fellow Christian?" Look for the heart that bears the fruit of a transformed life. Marry a person whose life displays the fruit of the Beatitudes. Look for the person who is not only poor and sad, but also for the person who has been tamed unto meekness by God's grace.

Do you see what God is doing? He is calling you to marry a person who exceeds the world's standard. Be honest: are poverty, sadness, and especially meekness found on your non-negotiable list? Perhaps you are wondering how meekness can be something good. Many think of meekness as weakness. It conjures up images of a person who is without conviction, cowardly, shy, wishy-washy, wimpy, and emotionally flabby. This is not the meekness that God produces in His people.

Who are the meek? The term *meek* comes from the Greek word, *praus,* that can best be translated as a person who is gentle. It bears none of the negative connotation that carries over into our modern understanding. The word is sometimes used interchangeably with humility. It is used four times in the New Testament (Matthew 5:5; 11:29; 21:5; 1 Peter 3:4) and is always translated "gentle" in the NASB. In classical Greek it was used to describe a wild animal that has been trained to come willingly under the control of its master.

Contrast this gentleness with the person who is stubbornly self-willed and lacks self-control. This is the person who is "like a city that is broken down, and without walls" (Proverbs 25:28). The natural man detests being numbered with the meek. Those who are not meek are the high-handed, self-assertive, demanding, harsh, vengeful, uncontrolled bullies of this world. Their hearts are too swelled with self to have any room for Christ, His Gospel, or those around them.

How will you recognize the meek? First and foremost, they will be those who display meekness toward God. They will accept God's way without murmuring. Here are several questions to ask:

Are They Surrendered to God's Sovereign Will?

Sometimes referred to as His "decretive will," God's sovereign will is the ultimate cause of all things (Psalm 115:3). God's decretive will refers to the secret, all-encompassing, divine purpose according to which He ordains everything that comes to pass. God does not always reveal this will to us, but leaves us to discover it when it actually comes to pass. Suddenly, His sovereign will is revealed when a child dies in infancy. His will is known when a lifetime of savings is lost at the crash of the stock market.

Our holy God has even decreed the consequences that spring from the sinful acts of mankind without Himself being the author of sin. In Genesis 50:20, Joseph told his brothers regarding their evil treatment of him, "But as for you, ye thought evil against me; *but* God meant it unto good, to bring to pass, as *it is* this day, to save much people alive." Remember, every event in your life finds its origin in the determinative will of God.

A meek person is willing to put himself under the adverse hand of God's providence. How do you know if a person's heart is meek? Observe how he responds to the trials and adversities of life. Listen for murmuring against God. Do you hear grumbling, like the Jews over manna in the wilderness (1 Corinthians 10:10)? Jonah's lack of meekness could be heard as he grumbled over a gourd plant that God sent to provide shade. God asked him, "Doest thou well to be angry for the gourd? And he said, I do well to be angry, even unto death" (Jonah 4:9). Such is the heart of the proud and defiant. The meek gently bows before a sovereign God who rules over all things perfectly.

Are They Surrendered to God's Revealed Will?

God's revealed will, also called His "preceptive will," encompasses all of the commands and precepts found in the Bible for our good and His glory. The meek have been graced with a submissive, teachable spirit to the Word of God. They are not know-it-alls. They know God is all-wise, and they come eagerly and humbly to be fed. They accept His law and precepts as good and therefore do not dispute or resist. James exhorts Christians to "receive with meekness the engrafted word, which is able to save your souls. But be ye doers of the word, and not hearers only, deceiving your own selves" (James 1:21-22). The heart of the meek is a heart of obedience to the commands of the King. God commands; the meek obey! He leads; they follow! They are pliable in the hands of God. They are no longer spiritually wild Mustangs. God has tamed them by His Spirit. They no longer rear up and resist the hand of God, but rather yield as He gently pulls on the reins of their hearts with His Word.

There are few greater blessings to a family than hearts that are mutually yielded to the Word of God. The home of the proud and self-willed will be misguided and filled with turmoil. The home of the meek will be filled with joyful harmony as family members humbly bow to God's will for their life together. The marriage of the meek will be biblically ordered and guided by the Word of God. The meek husband will lovingly lead his wife in the pathway of holiness. The meek wife will count it a joy to submit to the earthly head that was given to her by her Lord. A humble yielding to God's Word touches on every area of family life including roles of husbands and wives, family planning, patterns for raising and educating children, communication, prioritizing finances, proper recreation, as well as family and corporate worship of God.

You might be asking, "How can I know if the person I am courting is a person who receives God's Word in meekness?" The proud says, "My will be done." The meek humbly declare, "Thy will be done."

Look for the person who treasures the Word of God. You will see them open the Scriptures daily and devour them as food for the soul. The meek are the ones who realize that they do not have all the answers to life. The meek do not quarrel with God's Word. They do not deflect it when it is preached, but take it to heart.

Listen for the person to tell what he is learning or

how God is guiding him in new decisions based on the precepts of God's Word. We see the heart of meekness in Cornelius, who gathered with his family and friends to hear the Word of God brought by Peter (Acts 10:33). What a blessing meekness to God's Word brings to a marriage.

Are They Surrendered to Wise Discipline?

The writer to the Hebrews reminds us that God chastises everyone He loves. When under the rod of God, the meek will not kick and resist, but will yield with a heart of the peaceable fruit of righteousness. How does the person respond to the correcting hands of the authorities that God has placed in his life? Is he in rebellion to his parents? Does he mock his parents' correction? A daughter who stiffly rejects the headship of her father will be a wife who struggles to submit to her husband. Is this a person who is kicking defiantly against the legal system? Is he a member of a local church? Often, an unwillingness to join a local congregation reveals a heart that is unwilling to be accountable to others. Listen to the words of the meek, and you will hear them echo the Scriptures: "Furthermore we have had fathers of our flesh which corrected us, and we gave them reverence: shall we not much rather be in subjection unto the Father of spirits, and live?" (Hebrews 12:9).

Are They Surrendered to People?

A person who is meek towards God is a person who will also be meek towards man. Paul reminds Titus to teach the brethren "To speak evil of no man, to be no brawlers, *but* gentle, shewing all meekness unto all men" (Titus 3:2).

Dads, and those of you who are unmarried, look for a person who is not only submissive towards God, but who bears these two marks of meekness: forbearance and forgiveness.

Forbearance

The person who lacks meekness is a person with a heart in turmoil, churning like a stormy sea. This is the person who is overly defensive, argumentative, angry, and at times combative. But the subduing grace of God tames wild-hearted sinners and gives them a new heart of meekness that restrains them from a life of anger, malice, and revenge. Like Christ, he chooses to be longsuffering and forbears when wronged.

Think for a minute what a heart of unrestrained anger might mean to your marriage. Because the marriage union is the most intimate of relationships, it is one of the most fragile. The number of sparks that can ignite a heart of anger are limitless, whether it be a burned dinner, disheveled house, an absentee husband, rowdy kids, or upside down finances. Consider the person who forbears responding in anger. This is a person who does not have a short fuse. Your time of courtship should not be marked by anger and fighting. Don't ever marry a person who lashes out in fits of anger.

Listen for anger. Angry words can hurt worse than a knife wound. Listen for cutting words, ridicule, undue sarcasm, and name-calling. The meek will speak with words seasoned with grace.

Many a young lady wrongly thought that a combative courtship would somehow be transformed into marital bliss. When I first began practicing law, a young Christian lady came into my office to explore her legal options. She had been married less than two years. God had blessed her with a newborn son. With tears in her eyes, she shared how her husband would get off work, head to the bar, come home drunk, and use her for his punching bag. I asked her when this all began and she replied, "He's been that way as long as I've known him. I thought he would be better after we were married." It is true that we all can change by the grace of God, but don't marry based on that hope. Don't be tempted to think, "After we get married things will be better." They might not! A person is more likely to be forbearing prior to marriage. The day after the honeymoon is when the mask comes off and the true heart is revealed.

A malicious person is not a meek person. When anger continues unchecked, hearts become malicious and vindictive. Spontaneous outbursts of anger will turn to evil conniving against the other. Nothing rips a marriage apart like malice. Malice is a chainsaw that rips and tears apart the joy and unity that comes from being one flesh. Malice moves people to speak evil of their spouse to others. It is a malicious insomnia that keeps a spouse lying awake thinking of ways to hurt the one who is bone of their bones, flesh of their flesh.

I counseled a man who told me how his wife of thirty years had meticulously planned to take all of the family finances before she left him. She set up her own private account where all the paychecks were deposited. The bills remained unpaid for several months. Then the day she left, she withdrew the remaining balance in all of the checking and savings accounts. The meek are not malicious.

When malice goes unchecked, the heart often erupts in revenge. The natural man's heart repays evil with evil. Revenge stands in opposition to Christian love. Paul writes, "Dearly beloved, avenge not yourselves, but *rather* give place unto wrath: for it is written, Vengeance *is* mine; I will repay, saith the Lord" (Romans 12:19).

Beware of the person who repays evil with evil, who always seems aimed at getting even with those who wrong him. The meek do not seek revenge. A close friend shared with me a deep hurt that he had kept to himself for more than 20 years. The couple were not forbearing with one another. They battled off and on for years. Over the years, anger turned to malice. Finally, malice turned to revenge when his wife withdrew from the marriage bed, leaving her husband to a life of celibacy.

Forgiveness

Meekness does not stop at forbearance; it is also a heart attitude that is quick to extend forgiveness when wronged. Even the best of marriages are not sin-free. It is impossible this side of glory to love one another perfectly like Christ loves His bride. The key to a happy marriage is a willingness of the one guilty of a wrong to seek forgiveness, while the one wronged joyfully and quickly forgives, leading to the restoration of the marriage in the bond of love.

One of the greatest joys (and heartaches) of my ministry has been counseling couples on the verge of divorce. My private prayer throughout each counseling session is, "Lord, please do a work in each of their hearts to bring reconciliation for Your glory's sake!" There have been times when there seemed to be wonderful breakthroughs. Suddenly and powerfully, the Holy Spirit would lance the heart of a spouse. Their head would drop, and with tears streaming down their face, they would look to the other and confess, "I am so sorry. Will you forgive me?" At this point, I would be at the edge of my chair anticipating the words, "Yes, I forgive you!" Sadly, this has not always been the response. A reply that I have painfully heard more than once was, "I can't. I can't take it anymore." Translation: "I won't! I refuse to be meek! My own feeling of pain is greater than God's will. I love myself more than I am willing to love you. I'll take God's infinite forgiveness for my sins, but I have reached the limit of my forgiveness for yours!" It is this stubborn unwillingness to forgive that has led to many shattered marriages. Remember, forgiveness is Christ-like and knows no end (Matthew 18:21-22).

The meek not only forgive in word, but also in deed. They faithfully take all the steps necessary that lead to full reconciliation (Matthew 5:24). After all, loving acts of kindness and changed behavior do more than mere words to display a heart of true repentance.

Finally, the meek don't continue to harbor the wrongs of their spouse, but seek to forgive in thought as well. They don't say, "I forgive you," while at the same time replaying the wrong over and over again in their mind. By God's grace, the meek seek to align their thoughts with their words and deeds. They heed the words of the Apostle Paul: "Finally, brethren, whatsoever things are true, whatsoever things *are* honest, whatsoever things *are* just, whatsoever things *are* pure, whatsoever things *are* lovely, whatsoever things *are* of good report; if *there be* any virtue, and if *there be* any praise, think on these things" (Philippians 4:8).

This morning my wife Mary asked, "We've never had a fight during our marriage, have we?" I stopped and thought for a minute. Surely, after more than four decades of marriage, we must have had at least one fight. But, I couldn't think of one and neither could she. What a blessing it is to forget! Marry a person who forgives, forgets and returns good for evil.

Singles and Dads, look for the person who is meek. This will be the person who does not keep accounts of the wrongs of others. Beware of the person who has a history of broken relationships with parents, employers, relatives, and friends. You will often hear them blame the other person for these relationship wrecks. Ask yourself if they are forbearing. Are they quick to extend forgiveness in word, thought and deed?

The Promised Blessing of the Meek

There is a promised blessing to all who are meek. As with all the Beatitudes, meekness brings a blessed life of happiness. In the marriage of the meek, you will find a life of true abiding joy!

George Whitfield experienced the blessing of witnessing such happiness in the home of Jonathan and Sarah Edwards. Theirs was truly an uncommon marriage. He pictured Sarah Edwards as a wife "adorned with a *meek* and quiet spirit. She talked solidly of the things of God, and seemed to be such a helpmeet of her husband, that she caused me to renew those prayers…that He would be pleased to send me a daughter of Abraham to be my wife."[30]

Jesus adds a second amazing promise: "For they shall inherit the earth" (Matthew 5:5b). What does our Lord mean by inheriting the earth? This promise is again emphatic. It is as if Jesus is saying that the meek and only the meek shall inherit the earth. This is a blessing reserved to all who have been saved by grace. It is a promise of a present inheritance this side of glory. Perhaps Martyn Lloyd-Jones summarizes it best, "The meek already inherit the earth in this life, in this way. A man who is truly meek is a man who is already satisfied; he is a man who is already content. Goldsmith expresses it well when he says: 'Having nothing yet hath all.'"[31]

There is a future dimension to this promise as well. For the Christian, there will be a new heaven and a new earth. We will reign with Christ (Romans 8:17)! We will judge angels (1 Corinthians 6:3)! There are glories ahead

---

[30] *George Whitfield's Journals*, (London: Banner of Truth Trust, 1960), 472-477. Journal entry for October 19, 1740.
[31] Lloyd-Jones, *Studies in the Sermon on the Mount*, 59.

for the meek that are beyond our sanctified imaginations! Overflowing eternal joys without measure are yet ahead!

Let me close by giving you a perfect picture of what to look for in the person you marry. Marry a person like the Lord Jesus Christ. Jesus calls us to "Take my yoke upon you, and learn of me; for I am *meek* and lowly in heart: and ye shall find rest unto your souls" (Matthew 11:29). Puritan Thomas Watson reminds us to be imitators of Christ: "Christ does not bid us (says Augustine) learn of him to work miracles, to open the eyes of the blind, to raise the dead, but he would have us learn of him to be meek. If we do not imitate his life, we cannot be saved by his death."[32]

The omnipotent Lord Jesus Christ, very God, who powerfully spoke into being all of creation, entered this world *meekly* as a man, perfectly obedient to His heavenly Father. When He was interrogated by Pilate, He kept silent. As they mocked and spat upon Him, He did not retaliate. The glory of His meekness can be seen as He hung from the Cross, blood flowing from the open wounds from the steel spikes driven into his hands and feet. Suffocating under His own weight, he uttered, "Forgive them; for they know not what they do."

I would encourage you to put "Christ-like" at the top of your non-negotiable list. Look for the person who has been subdued by the gracious hand of the Master trainer. Marry the meek!

---

[32] Watson, *The Beatitudes*, 114.

Chapter 8

Marry the Hungry

Blessed are they which do hunger and thirst after righteousness: for they shall be filled.

- Matthew 5:6

It is not an accident that gas stations have morphed into convenience markets. We seem to get hungry about the time the gas gauge reads empty. A quick pit stop lets us grab a bag of chips and a can of Mountain Dew and race off with a full tank and a full belly. Our hunger, once again, is temporarily satisfied.

There are few urges that we feel as strongly as those of hunger and thirst. Most of us experience a daily hunger that is mild and short-lived, a friendly inward reminder that it is time to eat once again. Much of the world is not as blessed. According to the United Nations, there are more than one-billion chronically hungry people who have no drive-ins, convenience stores, or fridges to browse through. For them, hunger and thirst are strong, painful urges that are never satisfied.

Hunger and thirst can be understood more broadly as synonyms to describe any strong compelling craving or desire. Some hunger after power while others thirst for riches. Here our Lord borrows from the vocabulary of the physical realm to describe as blessed (or "happy") those who hunger and thirst after righteousness.

What's Inside

Before we explore the depth of this Beatitude, let's stop briefly and look at the unique order and structure of all eight Beatitudes. Remember, they are not listed haphazardly. Jesus lists them in an orderly progression. The first Beatitude is poor in spirit; the last is persecution. By design, both of these Beatitudes include this unique promise: "Theirs is the kingdom of heaven." These are like the two bookends between which each of the other Beatitudes is sandwiched.

Also notice that there are two groups of four Beatitudes. Both the first four and the second four end with references to "righteousness." The first four end with, "Blessed are those who hunger and thirst after *righteousness*" (v. 6), while the second four end with, "Blessed are they which are persecuted for *righteousness* sake" (v. 10).

The first three verses leading up to verse 6 each describe emptiness of self that precedes trusting in Christ. These are the three attitudes that God produces in the heart of the person He is saving. God initiates His work of salvation by first bringing the sinner to the end of himself. He must first be brought to see his sin debt as so high that it is impossible to ever repay it. This leads the spiritually bankrupt to not only sorrow, but to flee from their sins. God is not finished. This godly sorrow softens the heart with meekness so that the sinner is ready to humbly come to God on His terms. God now creates the spiritual hunger and thirst for what the empty soul so desperately needs: righteousness.

The Beatitudes end with a final reference to

righteousness. Here is the point: the righteousness that the sinner once hungered and thirsted for is given by God. He wonderfully imputes the righteousness of His Son to all whom He saves. Then, by the indwelling work of the Holy Spirit, the new Christian is empowered to grow in practical righteousness.

This progression of grace is important to help you discern God's will as to whom you should marry. Remember, as a Christian you are to marry another Christian. What are the marks of a true believer? There are many given in Scripture, but we have eight listed here in the opening verses of the Sermon on the Mount. Because they are progressive, we are not left to pick and choose from the Beatitudes. Marry the merry! Marry the person that has been adorned with all eight of these blessings from God.

Finally, although all eight of these graces will manifest themselves in the heart of a true believer, you will not find them perfectly present in any particular believer. Paul declares, "Therefore if any man be in Christ, he is a new creature: old things are passed away; behold, all things are become new" (2 Corinthians 5:17). New? Yes! Perfect? No! Don't look for perfection in the person you marry. Instead, look for a growing measure of each of these graces in his life.

Before we apply this Beatitude to marriage, we first must define three words: *hunger, thirst,* and *righteousness.* First, what does Jesus mean by hunger and thirst? Again, hunger is pain and a longing desire whereby the soul craves after what it does not have, righteousness. Spiritual thirst only intensifies this craving. Just as the parched and starving cannot live without bread and water, neither can parched and starving souls live without righteousness.

What is the meaning of righteousness? Righteousness in the Greek, *dikaiosune*, means to be properly right or fully justified according to all of God's requirements. In short, it carries the meaning of perfect conformity with the law of God. You might think of it as the opposite of sin, which is a breaking of the law. Jesus is describing a hunger and thirst after the very thing that none of us possess! Paul rightfully concludes, "As it is written, There is none righteous, no, not one" (Romans 3:10); "For all have sinned, and come short of the glory of God" (Romans 3:23). Jesus is describing a craving after being right with God! Being delivered from sin! Robert Murray M'Cheyne declares that it is hunger that cries out, "Oh God, make me as holy as a pardoned sinner can be!"[33] This was the thirst of David, "As the hart panteth after the water brooks, so panteth my soul after thee, O God. My soul thirsteth for God, for the living God: when shall I come and appear before God?" (Psalm 42:1-2).

This Beatitude comes with this promise: "They shall be filled" (v. 6b). All who hunger and thirst after righteousness "shall be filled" by God! There is a two-fold righteousness that comes from the gracious hand of God. First, there is the imputed righteousness of Christ. The bad news is that we are unrighteous sinners by nature. All of our attempts at righteous deeds are nothing more than filthy

---

[33] Andrew Murray, *Absolute Surrender and Other Addresses* (Chicago: Bible Institute Colportage Association, 1897), 108.

rags. There is nothing we can do to gain righteousness. But, there is good news.

There is One who is righteous, the Lord Jesus Christ (Jeremiah 23:6). He is the only One without sin—who perfectly kept the law of God. This is the glory of justification by faith. A wonderful transaction has taken place for all who have placed their trust in Christ alone and His death on the Cross as payment for their sins. Their sins were imputed to Christ! He not only became sin for them, but He sacrificially died for every one of them. God did not stop there! He imputed the righteousness of Christ to the sinner. This is the good news of 2 Corinthians 5:21 which says, "For he hath made him *to be* sin for us, who knew no sin; that we might be made the righteousness of God in him."

In the words of John Bunyan, "Our sins, when laid upon Christ, were yet personally ours, not his; so his righteousness, when put upon us, is yet personally his, not ours."[34] Through faith in Christ, we are justified. God extends His complete forgiveness and saves our soul! Paul victoriously declares, "Blessed is the man to whom the Lord will not impute sin" (Romans 4:8).

This hunger and thirst does not stop with justification. The justified are not satisfied to merely be forgiven by God; they continue to crave after holiness and Christlikeness! They hunger and thirst to be free from sin and to live lives of purity. It is the lifetime passion of every true Christian to be more and more like Jesus. Again, Jesus

---

[34] John Bunyan, *The Entire Works of John Bunyan*, ed. H. Stebbing (Oxford: Oxford University, 1859), 383.

promises, "They shall be filled." The Christian continues to grow in grace without fully reaching perfection this side of eternity. Through the new birth, God implants a new heart, and the sinner is given a divine nature (2 Peter 1:4). The Spirit of God comes to indwell the believer and does His daily work of sanctification powerfully, while the believer continues to hunger and thirst to be more like Christ.

Marry the hungry! Marry the person whose appetite and thirst crave for God to free them from their sins and passionately pursue a life of holiness! This raises a practical question: how do you know the appetite of the person you are courting? Simply look at what they are craving. How do you know a vegetarian? They turn from all meat and crave veggies. You might hear them cry out, "Give me collard greens or I will die!" Those who are hungering and thirsting after righteousness will crave after holiness, Christ, and the means of spiritual growth. Let's look at them:

Crave Holiness!

Look for the person who has no appetite for anything other than being right with God. You won't find them hungering and thirsting after the world with all its sinful attractions. Look at their life, and you will see a person who has a hatred for sin. They will not tempt you to compromise your purity. A close friend of mine in seminary courted and later married a young lady during our first school year. His one passion was to keep their relationship pure. He shared with me their commitment not to kiss each other until the day of their wedding. Each time they went out together, they first bowed in prayer, asking God to keep their thoughts and actions pure for the glory of God.

If you listen carefully to their words, you will hear their passion to be like Jesus! Listen for words seasoned with grace, words that speak often of Christ and are full of thanksgiving! Their treasure will not be found in this world, but in the kingdom of heaven.

Do not be deceived by counterfeits. There is a thirst and an appetite for self-righteousness that disguises itself as true righteousness. This is the appetite for religion without righteousness. Ever since Cain, mankind has tried to parade its own righteousness before God. This is the thirst and appetite of the Pharisees whom our Lord strongly condemned as hypocrites during His earthly ministry. It is a righteousness that says to God and others, "Look at me! Look what I just did!"

Many evangelical churches today are full of young people who have walked down an aisle, been baptized, regularly attend church, carry their Bible, pray prayers, enthusiastically raise their hands in praise, and even play their guitar in the worship band, but who know nothing of the righteousness of God.

Crave Christ!

As we have already seen, the person who is truly hungering and thirsting after righteousness realizes that his own righteousness is but filthy rags! There is only One, Jesus Christ, the Son of the living God, who is righteous!

He alone promises to clothe in His robe of righteousness all who trust in Him and His work on the Cross. The person who hungers and thirsts after righteousness is the person who flees from their sins and trusts in Jesus Christ as their Lord and Savior! The only righteousness in which they can boast is Christ's righteousness! Their sins are now forgiven and they are now adopted sons of God!

This is why a credible testimony of faith is so important in courtship. How do you know if a person is trusting in Christ alone for salvation? Listen carefully to their testimony. It is not uncommon for a person to become "twitterpated" with another before they discover that person's spiritual heart. By the time the conversation turns to spiritual matters, they are satisfied to hear them stumble over any words that sound "Christian." Listen and, if necessary, pry from them a credible testimony. Beware of words that trigger self-righteousness. They should be able to articulate their faith in Christ alone. They should have an awareness that their standing before God is not based on their righteousness, but the righteousness of Jesus Christ.

The "Prince of Preachers," Charles Spurgeon, realized the importance of such a credible testimony before he married his princess, Susannah Thompson, on January 8th, 1856. It might seem slightly formal by today's standards, but he kindly asked Susannah if she would give him a written confession of her repentance and faith in Jesus Christ. Her glad response must have been met with hearty approval as Spurgeon replied:

What's Inside

My Dearest,

The letter is all I can desire. Oh! I could weep for joy (as I certainly am doing now) to think that my beloved can so well testify to a work of grace in her soul. I knew you were really a child of God, but I did not think you had been led in such a path. I see my Master has been ploughing deep, and it is the deep-sown seed, struggling with the clods, which now makes your bosom heave with distress. If I know anything of spiritual symptoms, I think I know a cure for you. Your position is not the sphere for earnest labour for Christ. You have done all you could in more ways than one; but you are not brought into actual contact either with the saints, or with the sinful, sick, or miserable, whom you could serve. Active service brings with it warmth, and this tends to remove doubting, for our works thus become evidences of our calling and election.[35]

Crave a Means of Growth

A hunger and thirst to live a righteous and holy life creates a passion for the God-given means of growing in holiness. The person who hungers after earthly food has a passion for all the means that make that food table-ready. You will find them browsing the aisles of the supermarket, watching the cooking shows on PBS, as well as cooking in the kitchen or barbequing in the backyard. So too there will be a craving for the ordinary means through which the Holy

[35] Ray Charles, *The Life of Charles Spurgeon* (London: Passmore and Alabaster, 1903), 148.

Spirit sanctifies His people. What are the means that God uses to grow us in grace? A faithful gathering with God's people on the Lord's Day, the Word of God, prayer, and observance of the ordinances of baptism and the Lord's Supper.

Look for the person who is passionate about these means of grace. This will be a person who delights in the Lord's Day. You will find this person worshipping with the saints rather than surfing the waves on Sunday. They obey the writer to the Hebrews: "And let us consider one another to provoke unto love and to good works: Not forsaking the assembling of ourselves together, as the manner of some is; but exhorting one another: and so much the more, as ye see the day approaching" (Hebrews 10:24-25). They will order their work schedule and weekly activities to set aside one day in seven as the Lord's Day. They delight in hearing the preached Word. Their joy is found in singing hymns of praise to their Savior! Their faith is inflamed through remembrance of Jesus around the Lord's Table. David Brainerd, eighteenth century missionary to the New England Indians, describes such a time in his diary:

Lord's Day, Oct. 19, 1742. In the forenoon I felt my soul hungering and thirsting after righteousness. While I was looking on the sacramental elements, and thinking that Jesus Christ would soon be "set forth crucified before me," my soul was filled with light and love, so that I was almost in an ecstasy; my body was so weak, I could scarcely stand. I felt at the same time an exceeding tenderness and most fervent love toward all mankind; so that my soul and all the powers of it seemed, as it were, to melt into softness and sweetness. But during the communion, there was some abatement of this life and fervour. This love and joy cast out fear; and my soul longed for perfect grace and glory.[36]

The person hungering to be like Jesus will be a person who realizes he is what he is by the grace of God. He will not be a stranger to prayer. You will hear him giving thanks and asking God for His daily mercies. You will find yourself praying together as you seek God's will in courtship.

Look for a person, like David, who is hungering and thirsting after the Word of God. Examine the heart of the one you are courting in light of the following Scriptures:

O God, thou art my God; early will I seek thee: my soul thirsteth for thee, my flesh longeth for thee in a dry and thirsty land, where no water is. – Psalm 63:1

The fear of the Lord is clean, enduring for ever: the judgments of the Lord are true and righteous altogether. More to be desired are they than gold, yea, than much fine gold: sweeter also than honey and the honeycomb. – Psalm 19:9-10

This is the person who reads and knows God's Word. They will open the Scriptures with you and speak regularly of what God is teaching them! You will find yourself discussing together the meaning and application of the Word in your life.

---

[36] Jonathan Edwards, *The Works of Jonathan Edwards v. 2* (repr., Edinburgh: The Banner of Truth Trust, 1997), 320.

As with all the Beatitudes, this one comes with blessings! Not only will they be happy, but they will be "filled." Look at the wonder of grace! God first creates the hunger and thirst for righteousness in the soul. Then He fills the hungering and thirsting soul with the righteousness of His Son and continues to grow the believer in holiness!

Here is the wonder of sanctification. The more you hunger, the more He fills. It does not stop there! The more He fills, the more you hunger. And so it goes until the believer sees His Savior face to face! "We shall be like Him" (1 John 3:2), and then we shall hunger and thirst no more. We will gather at the marriage feast with our Savior! Thomas Watson comforts us with these words, "After your funeral begins your festival. Long for supper-time. 'The delay is long which separates us from our honey-sweet joys.' Christ has paid for this supper upon the cross, and there is no fear of a 'reckoning' to be brought in. 'Wherefore comfort one another with these words.'"[37]

---

[37] Watson, *The Beatitudes*, 104

Chapter 9

Marry the Merciful

Blessed are the merciful:
for they shall obtain mercy.

- Matthew 5:7

I joined in the toast of the best man as he raised his glass at the reception following my nephew Nate's wedding. He prefaced his toast by telling the gathered crowd how he and the groom had roomed together in college. He went on to give three reasons why he believed Nate would make an excellent husband. His number one reason came in the form of a story from their early college years. He described how one day the solitude of their apartment was suddenly rocked by loud cries from outside. "It sounded like an all-out brawl!" he exclaimed. He told how he quickly ran into the street, wondering if he might find Nate in the middle of the melee. Instead, to his surprise, out from the crowd came Nate with bandages and hydrogen peroxide in hand. This best man clearly understood the link between a heart of mercy and a happy marriage.

Who are the merciful? The Greek term for mercy encompasses feelings as well as actions. It springs from a heart of compassion or concern for people in need. It doesn't stop there. This feeling of compassion must spring into action to relieve the suffering or misery of the person in need. It is a heartfelt disposition to be an instrument of good. God commands us *to show* mercy. James warns, "For he shall have judgment without mercy, that hath *showed no mercy*; and mercy rejoiceth against judgment" (James 2:13).

One of the greatest examples of mercy is found in our Lord's parable of the Good Samaritan described in Luke 10:25-37. There we graphically see three aspects of true mercy in action.

Mercy Sees a Need

Mercy begins by seeing the needs of others. This requires the grace of being other-oriented and sensitive to the sufferings of others. The parable of the Good Samaritan shows us a man who has been beaten up and robbed. His bloody, naked body was lying along the side of a busy road. The religious priest and the Levite ignored him and walked by. They were soon followed by a Samaritan who *saw* the man in his distress (Luke 10:33a).

Blind, self-focused eyes cannot see the pains of others. Several years ago, our family was on vacation and we stopped to spend the night in Page, Arizona. In the heat of summer, we found a restaurant that served pizza outside. The place was packed with tourists who twirled spaghetti around their forks and nursed their cold beverages. While we were waiting for our pizza, one of my children gazed at the parking lot across the street and noticed two men beating and kicking another man in the head with their pointed cowboy boots. Even though this man lay limp on the ground like a bloody rag doll, the two men continued to relentlessly beat him.

What was even more tragic than the beating was the reaction of the crowd of tourists. Sadly, they casually kept twirling their spaghetti and sipping their sodas as they watched as if it was some sort of entertainment as the man was being beaten to death before their eyes.

Mercy Is Moved by the Need

Mercy does not stop at seeing; it *feels* the needs of others. Jesus tells us that the Good Samaritan "had compassion on him" (v. 33b). The Samaritan's heart *felt* the painful suffering and abandonment that the victim was going through. While a callous world mocks, condemns, or coldly ignores the hurts of others, the merciful share in the pain and sorrow of those whom are hurting.

As our family watched the beating across the street, our collective hearts cried out for this man being beaten! We felt his helpless condition. We felt the pain of every blow to his head.

Mercy Moves to Meet Need

You can see a need and feel a need and still fall short of showing true mercy. Mercy takes one more important step. It reaches out to alleviate the distress. Unlike the religious leaders, the Samaritan poured wine and oil on the suffering man's open wounds before wrapping them in bandages. He picked up the man, put him on the back of his donkey, and took him to a nearby inn to recuperate at the Samaritan's expense (Luke 10:34-35).

Mercy acts! At the risk of being late, it stops in the midst of a busy schedule. When there is little, it digs deep in the pocket book to pay for the needs of others. It visits, cleans, binds wounds, calls, sends cards, goes, helps, and does for the needs of others.

As our family continued to watch this man being ruthlessly kicked, I could sit still no longer. I jumped up and grabbed the waiter and commanded him, "Call 911! Tell them to send the police and an ambulance—NOW!"

He casually replied, "No, it won't do any good; that kind of thing happens all the time around here."

The next thing I remember was my son and myself bolting out of our chairs and heading straight for the men across the street. I never stopped to think what I was going to do with the two guys who had murder in their eyes. All I knew was that I had to do something before this man died. Thankfully, the Lord intervened first. Sirens could be heard in the air, and as I arrived, the two men ran away. I learned later that the beaten man survived, but was left with permanent brain damage.

The greatest example of mercy is found in our Lord, Jesus Christ. Jesus concludes this Beatitude with a promise of mercy to all who are *merciful*. The merciful, and they alone, shall receive mercy. God is not a proponent of karma. This is not another form of *what goes around comes around*. Christians can only bestow mercy because they have first been recipients of mercy from the God of mercy

(2 Corinthians 1:3). In mercy, God sees us in our sinful state. He *sees* us as rebels under His wrath and waiting His ultimate judgment. In mercy God *feels* compassion towards us in our sinful state. His compassion becomes *active* by sending forth His Son to be the sin-bearer of His people by suffering the pains of the Cross. What mercy it is that would bear His Father's wrath that we might have forgiveness and everlasting life. If you have experienced His salvation, you are a living object of His mercy.

Paul writes of this mercy to the Ephesians:

"But God, who is rich in mercy, for his great love wherewith he loved us, Even when we were dead in sins, hath quickened us together with Christ, (by grace ye are saved;). And hath raised us up together, and made us sit together in heavenly places in Christ Jesus: That in the ages to come he might shew the exceeding riches of his grace in his kindness toward us through Christ Jesus" *(Ephesians 2:4-7).*

All who have received mercy will show mercy to others and will continue to receive mercy from God.

Marry the merciful. Marry the person who has received the mercy of God as evidenced by the fruit of showing mercy to others. This raises these questions: "How can you know if a person is merciful? What fruit will be on display?

Consider the person who is:

What's Inside

#1 – Merciful Towards Lost Sinners

The self-righteous condemn sinners and fail to see their lost estate. The merciful look around and *see* lost sinners. Everywhere they turn, they see souls enslaved to sin. They *feel* the pains caused by the ravages of sin. They hurt when sinners are arrested, feel pity when their marriages break up, and sorrow when others are struck with sin-caused disease. But above all, they feel anguish as they witness sinners moving headlong into the eternal wrath of God. You will hear them speak of their pity for the lost.

The merciful can't stop at feeling pity for sinners. True mercy must spring into action. Listen and you will hear the merciful speak up for their Lord! You will hear them joyfully proclaim His Gospel! The merciful grab the lifeline of the Gospel and cast it far and wide to drowning souls.

#2 – Merciful Towards the Physical Sufferings of Others

This will be the person who is other-oriented and sensitive to the suffering of those around him and quick to reach out with helping hands.

It might be a person like Jerry Graham, who was an ex-con saved in prison by the grace of God. Early in my Christian walk, Jerry joined me one Lord's Day to preach the Gospel at our local county jail. The word spread widely that Jerry was coming, and the meeting room was packed. During the preaching, an older prisoner in the front row showed obvious signs of frustration as he tried to read his pocket Gideon's Bible, holding it inches from his face. After the service, Jerry went to the man and asked him if he could read. "I can read; I want to read the Bible," he replied, "but I can't see! My glasses broke several months ago!"

Feeling the agony of this man's blindness and without batting an eye, Jerry took off his own glasses and said, "Here man, try these."

The inmate put on Jerry's glasses and shouted, "I can see!"

"Cool man," Jerry responded, "Keep them! I can always get another pair."

The person who is merciful will be a person who:

1. Responds generously to those who are poor and needy. It's the unmerciful who tells them to go be warmed and be filled and does nothing else.

2. Gives generously with his time and money for the needs of God's people. He sees himself as only a steward of the blessings God has bestowed upon him. He does not make excuses for why he doesn't give.

In conclusion, how important is it that you marry the merciful? It is a matter of marrying equally or being unequally yoked. Those whom God has been merciful towards have been graced with mercy. Finally, it is a matter of a blessed marriage or one that is cursed. The promise of blessing not only extends to the merciful, but to his family (Psalm 37:26).

Who should you marry? May God give you discernment to marry the merciful. Our Lord doesn't stop here. There are three more Beatitudes to consider. D. Martyn Lloyd-Jones describes the next Beatitude as "undoubtedly one of the greatest utterances to be found anywhere in the realm of Holy Scripture."[38]

---

[38] Lloyd-Jones, *Studies in the Sermon on the Mount*, 90.

Chapter 10

Marry the Pure

Blessed are the pure in heart:
for they shall see God.

- Matthew 5:8

One of our little granddaughters was just learning her alphabet in homeschool when she handed her mom a note that cryptically read, "MOMMY I ♥ YOU!" Children learn very early the relationship between the heart and love. From its root in paganism and mythology, the heart has become the modern symbol of love. A popular way of saying, "I love you," is with the gift of a heart-shaped card or box of chocolates.

However, not all hearts bring happiness and blessing to your marriage. In fact, there is a heart that can be hazardous to your marriage. The difference is not the shape, but the spiritual condition. What kind of heart is it that can bring blessing? Our Lord supplies the answer in this Beatitude: "Blessed are the pure in heart."

What does Jesus mean by a pure heart? Sometimes the *heart* is used synonymously with the emotions. If you can't decide between a pickup truck and a Prius, the car dealer might tell you to trust your heart. Let your feelings be your guide. That is why the heart has become associated with the *feelings* of love and passion for another. Our Lord's use of the word *"heart"* (*kardia*) runs much deeper than an emotional goose bump. It refers to the deep recesses of the inner self. Sometimes, it has been defined as the seat of one's personality. It encompasses the whole self, which includes will, affections, mind, and conscience. The heart is the real inner you that only God (not even you) ever truly knows (1 Samuel 16:7).

Since the fall of man back in Genesis 3, the heart of man has been corrupt and polluted by sin. From Adam taking his first sinful bite of the forbidden fruit until the first raindrop fell on the ark, God concluded that the wickedness of man was universally great. Even their inner thoughts that came from their hearts were always evil (Genesis 6:5). Scripture later reaffirms God's diagnosis that the heart of man is full of evil and madness (Ecclesiastes 9:3). Think of the heart as a deep well that has been tapped into the sewer. It produces nothing but the smelly sludge of sin. Jesus describes this defilement later in Matthew: "But those things which proceed out of the mouth come forth from the heart; and they defile the man. For out of the heart proceed evil thoughts, murders, adulteries, fornications, thefts, false witness, blasphemies" (Matthew 15:18-19).

None of Adam's fallen race can clean their own hearts. Sin not only defiles, but enslaves the heart to sin. That is why man's greatest need is for a complete heart transplant. There is no other hope! The good news is that God made a new covenant: "But this shall be the covenant that I will make with the house of Israel; After those days, saith the LORD, I will put my law in their inward parts, and write it in their hearts; and will be their God, and they shall be my people" (Jeremiah 31:33). He doesn't stop there; He promises a transplant: "A new heart also will I give you, and a new spirit will I put within you: and I will take away the stony heart out of your flesh, and I will give you an heart of flesh" (Ezekiel 36:26).

This brings us to the Gospel. Through the shed blood of Jesus Christ, this new covenant was ratified. Ponder these wonderful words of our Lord just before going to His bloody death on the Cross: "This cup is the new testament in my blood, which is shed for you" (Luke 22:20). God not only forgives, but He does what He has promised to do: He imparts a new heart to all who have been brought to trust in Jesus Christ as Savior and Lord— not just another heart, but a pure heart!

Having seen the corruption that flows from the hard, wicked heart of man, Jesus now puts on full display the purity of the new heart. What does Jesus mean by "pure in heart"? Our word "pure" comes from the Greek word *katharos,* which in a physical sense carries the meaning of clean, free from dirt, unsoiled, spotless, and free from any impure mixture. It was used to describe silver ore mixed with lead or tin that was placed in a refiner's fire to produce pure silver. This is not just sterling silver, 92.5% pure; it is 100% pure silver.

Jesus is carrying that same concept into the spiritual realm. The pure in heart describes all who have been born again. By grace, God has taken out the cold, dead heart of stone and replaced it with a pure heart of flesh. Now, the inward mind, will, conscience, and affections are singularly focused on holiness. In other words, every true Christian has been given a new heart that is pure in thought, affections, and will. It is not a heart that is hypocritical. It is the fountain from which all outer actions flow. D. Martyn Lloyd-Jones gives us this brief definition: "But perhaps we can perfectly express it by saying that being pure in heart means to be like the Lord Jesus Christ Himself, 'who did no sin, neither was guile found in his mouth' – perfect and spotless and pure and entire."[39]

Don't expect the pure heart to produce a perfectly pure life this side of eternity. It is a heart that beats after holiness, but it is tucked inside a fleshly body of sin. That is why the Christian life is one of warfare, where the believer is constantly engaged in daily spiritual battle for purity. The pure in heart are growing in grace and progressively becoming more Christ-like.

If you can't see this new inward heart, you might ask, "How can I know if the heart of the person I am courting is pure?" That's a great question to which there is no easy answer. Remember, you will never truly know your own heart, let alone the heart of another (Jeremiah 17:9). However, with much prayer, counsel, and spiritual discernment, you can discover much about the heart condition of the person you are considering for marriage.

Although you can't look on the inside, you can learn much about the heart from spoken words and the manner of a person's life. Remember, the heart is like a deep well. You might not be able to see what is at the bottom of it, but you can learn much from what comes out at the pump. A pure heart pumps out a pure life. A polluted heart produces a polluted life. You will learn much as you listen to the words and observe the actions of a person.

---

[39] Lloyd-Jones, *Studies in the Sermon on the Mount*, 95.

These become the windows into their heart (Matthew 7:17-27). Scripture gives us a partial checklist of polluted fruit that flows from an impure heart: "Evil thoughts, adulteries, fornications, murders, thefts, covetousness, wickedness, deceit, lasciviousness, an evil eye, blasphemy, pride, foolishness" (Mark 7:21-22).

It is the God-given role of the father to probe the heart of the suitor for purity. Don't make the mistake of confusing it with outward morality. Let me encourage you to peel back the outer veneer of religion and search the motives and the intent of the heart.

Several years ago, a young man asked if he could begin pursing God's will regarding marriage to one of my daughters. Before I answered him, we entered into several lengthy conversations about his personal testimony, walk with God, and where he thought God was leading him in life. Right in the middle of our discussion about his schooling, I stopped and, completely out of context, looked him right in the eye and interjected this question: "Tell me about your struggles with pornography." I was purposely attempting to catch him with his guard down. I was soliciting a spontaneous response that might expose a little more of his heart.

Without a hem or a haw, he quickly answered, "Like all men I've been tempted with pornography. But so far, God has been gracious to give me the strength to resist. I can honestly say that God has given me the strength to keep my eyes away from any pornographic magazines or websites."

Not only did I get a glimpse of his heart, but it

opened up a good conversation about the importance of maintaining a pure heart. A few months later, I gave my daughter to this young man. At a recent family gathering, he turned to me and said, "I'll never forget that question you asked me about pornography!" I hope it will be a lifelong reminder to maintain purity throughout his married life.

Dads, if you are going to discern a pure heart, you must pick up the magnifying glass and become a good detective. Engage the suitor in many conversations and listen carefully to his words. If a person talks enough, you will begin to hear your way into their heart. Listen for words of love for Christ and others. Do you hear a passion for worship and service, or do you hear words that are impure, covetous, foolish, proud, or hypocritical? Ask to be Facebook friends. For some reason, people will write and post things on Facebook that they would never tell you in person. I have known young men and young ladies who seemed to be the picture of Christian purity at church whose Facebook pages were defiled with filthiness. Their profile, friends and pictures will help you probe below the epidermal layer of religion.

Should you give permission for a young man to court your daughter, set clear guidelines for the courtship that will promote purity in the relationship. This should include a frank discussion about the importance of maintaining sexual purity. I believe it is the father's role to define the boundaries of physical contact throughout the courtship. What about holding hands or kissing? Should dating be limited to group activities?

I write these words believing that there is a degree of Christian liberty in setting the parameters of physical contact during a courtship. Obviously, any form of sexual intimacy prior to marriage is fornication and prohibited by God. I have known good Christian families who draw the line differently on hand holding and kissing prior to marriage. These are matters best left for fathers to determine.

However, if a couple is pure in heart and desires to keep their courtship pure, I believe a good case can be made for withholding the first kiss until the close of the marriage ceremony. Kissing is a level of intimacy that can inflame the passions of the flesh and weaken the resolve to resist increased sexual intimacy. I know that to the twenty-first century ear this view carries with it a ring of antiquity. However, it wasn't that long ago when serious Christian couples took strong measures in their resolve to preserve purity.

Let me take you back to Wheaton College. The year was 1948. Elisabeth Howard, a New Testament Greek major, was attracted to a handsome broad-chested fellow student, Jim Elliott, later a missionary to Ecuador and martyr at the hands of the Auca Indians. Elisabeth had learned of some prior kissing incidents involving Jim and a few young ladies. What does a girl with a pure heart do with such news? She went to Jim and confronted him with his prior indiscretions before marriage. Listen to Jim's heart in his reply:

I stood there, said and did as you have told me, entirely in the flesh. And the same "me" wrote of "purity in love." You may judge which, whether flesh or spirit, prompted me in this latter. For the fact that it has blackened my conscience, hurt you, stumbled others, and brought dishonor to Christ, I now experience overwhelming sorrow. The act, the effect of it, the regret for it shall be consumed by the flashing of my Judge's eye, and I shall suffer loss. There's an end of it, and a costly one. [40]

It breaks my heart that I can't encourage you through the example of my own dating experience. My wife and I were two lost sinners when God saved us seven years after we were married. However, I leave you with the example of a close seminary friend of mine who was courting a young lady, now his wife. They were a couple with pure hearts who wanted to pursue marriage God's way. They covenanted together from day one that they would not kiss until after they exchanged their marriage vows. Before they would go anywhere together, they would first bow their heads and ask God to strengthen them to maintain purity in their relationship for the glory of God. The purity of that first kiss at their wedding was not only pleasing to God, but a strong testimony of His grace to the groom's unbelieving family!

Provide many opportunities for the courting couple to get to know each other through family gatherings. Actively plan movie nights, lunch after church, picnics, and even work projects around the house. Remember, the more contact you have, the more glimpses you get of a person's

[40] Elisabeth Elliott, *Passion and Purity*, (1984; reprint, Grand Rapids: Revell, 2002), 136.

heart. During the courtship of one of my daughters, we encouraged the young man to spend as much time as he wanted at our house. He took us up on our offer and became a part of the Thomas clan. To protect my daughter's purity, we gave him this ground rule: When Mom and Dad go to bed, it's time to go home.

I have been speaking mostly to dads, but I want to reach the heart of each of you single readers pursuing God's will in marriage. Young ladies, it is one thing for your parents to defend your purity; it is another thing for you to share their same passion. A chaste relationship should be the desire of your pure heart. Be thankful for parents who love you enough to set boundaries, but make it your delight to keep those boundaries. If your parents choose to be disengaged in your courtship, set and keep your own boundaries before you are married.

The husband with a pure heart is a man of God who will love his wife with a love that leads her into the pathway of purity (Ephesians 5:25-26). Likewise, young men, if you have been graced with a pure heart, it will be your passion to use all the will and strength that God gives you to protect and promote a young lady's purity. Pray the following together as our Lord taught: "Lead us not into temptation." Avoid both places and people that might provoke compromise.

Let me add a word of warning to single ladies. Beware of the man who tempts you to compromise your purity. He might come to you with words like, "It's okay; it's natural," or "After all, sex is a gift from God," or "Why wait? We love each other and are going to get married soon."

The church of our day finds itself wading in the deep waters of spiritual compromise. It is walking in a cadence that is in step with the world. Fornication is rapidly becoming the latest sin to be added to a long list of so-called "respectable sins." A recent survey of 2,700 singles across the United States surprisingly revealed that 85% agreed that sex before marriage is now acceptable. What about Christian singles? Sadly, the same survey found professing Christians not far behind, with 84% admitting that they would live with a partner before marriage.[41] Resist the lips of the tempter who seductively suggests, "This is the twenty-fist century—everyone is doing it." Heed the words of the apostle Paul, "Flee fornication" (1 Corinthians 6:18)!

Young ladies, realize what a rich treasure you will be when you present yourself to your husband, pure and chaste. Again, Elisabeth Elliott brings some strong, practical, personal words of wisdom for all who purpose to be pure.

I wanted to marry a man prepared to swim against the tide. I took it for granted that there must be a few men left in the world who had that kind of strength. I assumed that those men would also be looking for women of principle. I did not want to be among the marked-down goods on the bargain table, cheap because they'd been pawed over. Crowds collect there. It is only the few who will pay

---

[41] http://www.online.wsj.com/article/PR-CO-20130122-906649.html

full price. 'You get what you pay for.'[42]

As we just witnessed from the life of Jim Elliott, even the pure in heart sin. Our perfected purity does not come until that glorious day when we see our Lord face to face. If you fall short during your courtship, flee to Christ for forgiveness. Don't let one act of disobedience become an excuse for greater sin.

A young man asked to meet with the father of the young lady he was courting. With his head dropped into his lap and tears streaming down his face, the young man confessed that he and the daughter had yielded to temptation and had violated the purity of their relationship. He confessed his sin against God, the daughter, and her father and asked the father if he could find room in his heart to forgive him. The father replied, "Our God is a faithful God who promises to forgive and cleans from all unrighteousness every one of His children who confesses his sins (1 John 1:9). I too forgive you." The young man eagerly agreed to adhere to the father's added steps to shield his daughter's purity.

Where there are pure hearts, there you will find happy marriages, but I must warn you, the converse is also true. Where there are impure hearts, there you will find families that are sad and filled with pain. Where there is impurity, there is heartache. I am close to four families whose marriages recently ended in divorce because of impure hearts. One man carried on a covert adulterous relationship with a fellow employee. In the second family, the wife indulged her adulterous heart with online

---

[42] Elliott, *Purity and Passion*, 129.

relationships. The third situation involved a wife who suddenly left her husband and son, without notice, to live with another man. Finding a former sweetheart online and cultivating a virtual relationship destroyed the fourth family.

These four couples were all professing Christians who were faithful members of doctrinally sound churches. They all joyfully sang praises to Christ each Lord's Day. All were active in Christian service. They were deacons, Sunday school teachers, pianists, and Bible study leaders. Like whitewashed tombs, they seemed so "Christian" on the outside, but their hearts were impure, like dead men's bones. Each of these marriages was ripped apart by divorce. Each left behind its own tragic trail of broken hearts, failed jobs, financial calamity, and worst of all, broken children.

Your marriage does not have to be added to the divorce statistics. Where pure hearts yoke themselves together, you will find happy marriages. These are the strong, faithful families built on the love of Christ. These are families where husbands and fathers make it their passion to pursue and protect the holiness of their wives and children from the sinful pressures of a fallen world. Their sole delight is found in eternal things rather than the things of this world that are perishing. These are families that are blessed to taste a little of heaven this side of eternity.

This Beatitude closes with one of the most amazing promises of blessing found anywhere in Scripture: "Blessed are the pure in heart: for they shall see God." The pure in heart are eternally happy. Purity is the only jewel you will be able to take with you when you die. Everything else will be given away, sold at a garage sale, or burned up as dross. In fact, those who are pure in heart will experience the ultimate purity in the presence of their Lord: "They (and they alone), shall see God."

You might ask, "How will we ever see God? Is He not an invisible Spirit (John 4:24)? Does not Paul tell us that no man has seen God (1 Timothy 6:16)? Do we not echo this truth when we sing, "Immortal *invisible*, God only wise"? It is true; God is a Spirit and therefore is invisible to the human eye. We will never see the embodiment of our heavenly Father or Holy Spirit until heaven. However, Jesus, the second person of the Trinity, is God, and He declares: "He that hath seen me hath seen the Father" (John 14:9). We see Jesus here and now in His Word, church, and the lives of His people. However, there is coming a day when the pure in heart shall see Him in all of His glory (1 John 3:2)! We can join with Isaac Watts and sing the praises of this great blessing:

Blest are the pure, whose hearts are clean
From the defiling powers of sin;
With endless pleasure they shall see
A God of spotless purity.[43]

Are you experiencing the happiness that comes to all whose hearts have been purified by the grace of God? Is it your passion that your marriage overflows with this same happiness? When two pure hearts are joined together as one

---

[43] "The Beatitudes" (No. 527 in . in Trinity Hymnal (Rev. ed.) (Suwanee, GA: Great Commission Publications, 1990).

flesh, God blesses that union with happiness. Even if the Beatitudes stopped here, there would be a lifetime of happiness in the heart and home of every believer in Christ, but God's grace is a super-abundant grace! It keeps cascading with blessing after blessing, beyond what we deserve or imagine. There is more! Jesus continues to build on this happiness with the next surprising Beatitude.

Chapter 11

Marry a Peacemaker

Blessed are the peacemakers:
for they shall be called the children of God.

- Matthew 5:9

Jerry was a close friend as well as a brother in Christ. Our backgrounds were different; I was a lawyer and he was a salesman. We attended different churches. But we had one thing in common—we were both peacemakers with hearts that longed to reach prisoners in our county jail with the liberating Gospel of Jesus Christ. Some of my fondest memories are of jumping into Jerry's pickup after church on Sunday and heading off to jail. I can still hear the heavy steel doors slamming automatically behind us, sealing us in our chapel bunker. Jerry and I would rotate preaching from week to week. Our prayer was that the Gospel would reverberate off the concrete walls into the hearts of the inmates. What a blessing it was to see murderers forgiven and drug addicts transformed through this Gospel outreach. Little did I know that God was stirring in both of our hearts a calling to the Gospel ministry.

Filled with a passion for the lost, Jerry and I sought the counsel of our elders and began to earnestly pray together for God's will about leaving our jobs and moving to southern California to attend seminary. Our faith was being challenged. We each shared with our wives how God had been leading us. My wife, Mary, and I prayerfully counted the cost. I remember telling her that we would have to sell our house and my law practice to pay for seminary. It well could be that we would never own a home again. Finally, we would have to find a new home for Brandy, our Saint Bernard. Mary responded by saying, "If that's where God is leading you, that's where He is leading our family." I thanked the Lord for a wife who was willing to trust in God's leading.

Jerry met with his wife, Martha, and shared his passion to give his life for the preaching of the Gospel. He assured her that God would provide for their family as they sought first His kingdom and righteousness. He then asked Martha, "Are you with me?"

Sadly, Martha was not a peacemaker. She stubbornly replied, "No! This is my town. These are my friends and my family. This is my house! We have worked hard to buy it and fix it up just the way we wanted it. No! I'm staying right here!"

Shortly thereafter, my family loaded up the U-Haul and headed off to seminary, without Brandy. Jerry and Martha stayed behind in their cute little ranch-style house. But that's not the end of the story. Less than a month following Martha's refusal to follow Jerry, fire engines could be heard screaming down their idyllic street. God would have the last word in the matter. Jerry and Martha's house was on fire. The firefighters did their best to save the home, but nothing was left but a charred concrete foundation. This tragedy underscores the importance of being, as well as marrying, a peacemaker.

As we closed the last chapter with God's blessing on the pure in heart, we are reminded that Jesus is chronologically building on each of the Beatitudes. All who are pure in heart (v. 8) become peacemakers (v. 9) who can expect to find themselves persecuted (v. 10-12). These links help unlock the meaning of this seventh Beatitude.

Observe how *purity* and *peace* are frequently listed as Siamese twins in Scripture. "Follow peace with all men, and holiness*"* (Hebrews 12:14). "But the wisdom from above is first pure, then peaceable" (James 3:17). God-given peace comes to the believer who is pure in heart. Those who have received peace want to extend that peace to others. Simply stated, all who are pure in heart have been made to be peacemakers.

What does Jesus mean by *peacemaker?* The meaning is narrowed as we consider some of the words that our Lord chose not to use. Notice that Jesus did not say blessed are the peace lovers, conflict-evaders, peaceniks at any cost, but 'Blessed are the peacemakers." *Peacemaker* is a compound word in the original Greek, *eirenopoios* (peace + make). We might expand the meaning to describe one who facilitates the binding together of those who are divided, thus working to make them one.

Ever since the Fall in Genesis 3, all of mankind has been without peace. In our wickedness, we were enemies of God (Isaiah 48:22; Romans 5:10; 8:7; Colossians 1:21). Unlike His fallen creation, our God is a God of peace (Romans 15:33; 1 Corinthians 14:33; Hebrews 13:20). The ultimate display of His grace is seen in His sending of His

Son, the Prince of Peace, into this world. His shed blood satisfied the wrath of God as He purchased peace for all who would trust in Him (Isaiah 9:6; Ephesians 2:14; Colossians 1:19-20).

All who by God's grace are poor in spirit, mourning over their sins, meek, hungering and thirsting after righteousness, merciful, and pure in heart now have peace with God. The war is over! God also graces them with an inward disposition of peace and contentment. The heart of the lost is like a stormy sea, constantly in a state of turmoil (Isaiah 57:20). The children of God have inward peace, knowing that their God is a loving Father who meets every one of their needs by His endless mercies. They also have full assurance that they have been saved and can lay their heads on the pillow each night in peace (Galatians 5:22).

In what way have we become peacemakers? What kind of peace are we to make? Who are the warring parties with whom we are to help facilitate a truce? How do we reconcile this Beatitude with our Lord's declaration that He didn't come to send peace to the earth, but instead to send a sword (Matthew 10:34)?

There is a sense in which all who have experienced the peace of God are to be active in making peace with others. The Christian life is not a life of fighting, bickering, strife and division. Instead, the scriptural directive is to do everything possible to live in peace with everyone (Romans 12:18). The writer to the Hebrews admonishes us to pursue peace with everyone, and holiness in our personal lives or we will never see God (Hebrews 12:14). In other words, the Christian is one who is not a fighter. When he is wronged, he is patient and longsuffering. The peacemaker prays for and does good to his enemies. When he wrongs others, he quickly seeks forgiveness and reconciliation.

Can you see how this kind of peacemaker brings happiness to the home? A home filled with combat and strife is a home that cannot survive. In fact, "*It is* better to dwell in the corner of the housetop, than with a brawling woman and in a wide house" (Proverbs 25:24; 19:13). How many children lay in bed at night listening to the bickering of their screaming parents?

During your courtship, look for the person who is at peace with those around him. What is his relationship with co-workers, family, and friends? How does the person treat you? Do your conversations often end in contentious arguments and verbal combat? In premarital counseling, I warn young ladies that if the man they are engaged to is verbally or physically abusive, "Don't marry him!"

I recently counseled with a couple whose honeymoon had barely come to an end. The wife characterized their first two months of marriage as nonstop combat. I asked her if she had seen any signs of a combative spirit in her husband before they were married. She answered, "Yes, there were signs, but I thought things would be better after our wedding." Don't be tempted to think that you will be the one who changes him after your marriage. Remember, the best foot is being put forward before you say, "I do."

As important as relational peacemaking is to the Christian walk, I believe our Lord is describing a peacemaking that is even loftier than mending earthly relationships. It is a peacemaking that actively seeks to reconcile sinners with their God. Jesus is extending the blessings of happiness to those who throw the lifeline of the Gospel to the unsaved. Peacemakers are those who have been graced with the heart of evangelism. The eyes of the peacemaker see the lost, sinful state of humanity. His heart is filled with mercy as he feels the painful consequences of their sins and the impending judgment that lies ahead. He hears with ears of faith His Lord's commission to go and make disciples. He is not content for his feet to remain fixed and his lips mute. The peacemaker goes, and broadcasts the Good News of the Cross to all whom God brings into his life. He is the Christian ambassador that Paul describes:

> *And all things are of God, who hath reconciled us to himself by Jesus Christ, and hath given to us the ministry of reconciliation; To wit, that God was in Christ, reconciling the world unto himself, not imputing their trespasses unto them; and hath committed unto us the word of reconciliation. NOW then we are ambassadors for Christ, as though God did beseech you by us: we pray you in Christ's stead, be ye reconciled to God.* – 2 Corinthians 5:18-20

You might object, saying, "Wait a minute; I'm not seeking to marry a missionary or a pastor. I just want to marry an ordinary Christian husband or wife. Why is it important that the person I marry have a heart of evangelism?" The answer to this question prompts another question, "What do you mean by ordinary Christian?" The scriptural definition of an ordinary Christian is much different than the average pew-sitter today. The ordinary Christian is a disciple of Jesus Christ. He has denied himself and picked up his cross to follow His Lord. Our Lord's final commission to "make disciples" (Matthew 28:19-20) was made to ordinary Christians. It is the ordinary Christian who is ready at a moment's notice to tell another of their hope in Christ (1 Peter 3:15).

The presence or absence of this Beatitude will be the difference between happiness and heartache in the family. Happy is the home where both parents are peacemakers. This is a home in which parents will labor together for the souls of their children. Mom and Dad will faithfully bring to bear all of the ordinary means of grace for their salvation. This will be the family where parents persevere in praying for the conversion of their children. The family will worship together through daily devotions, bringing the Gospel regularly before their hearts.

John Payton, a nineteenth century missionary to the New Hebrides, was raised by a father who was a peacemaker. He was a dad who cried out to God, not only for the souls of his eleven children, but also that God might be pleased to call them to the ministry of the Gospel. He was blessed to see his prayers answered as three of his sons were called to the ministry of Christ. John Payton fondly reminisces about growing up with a father who was a peacemaker:

> *Each of us, from very early days, considered it no penalty, but a great joy, to go with our father to the church; the four miles were a treat to our young spirits, the company by the way was a fresh*

incitement, and occasionally some of the wonders of city-life rewarded our eager eyes...and when these God-fearing peasants "foregathered" in the way to or from the House of God, we youngsters had sometimes rare glimpses of what Christian talk may be and ought to be...I have to bear my testimony that religion was presented to us with a great deal of intellectual freshness, and that it did not repel us but kindled our spiritual interest. The talks which we heard were, however, genuine; not the make-believe of religious conversation, but the sincere outcome of their own personalities. That, perhaps, makes all the difference betwixt talk that attracts and talk that drives away...We had, too, special Bible Readings on the Lord's Day evening, — mother and children and visitors reading in turns, with fresh and interesting question, answer, and exposition, all tending to impress us with the infinite grace of a God of love and mercy in the great gift of His dear Son Jesus, our Saviour. The Shorter Catechism was gone through regularly, each answering the question asked, till the whole had been explained, and its foundation in Scripture shown by the proof-texts adduced...How he would entice us to help him to recall some idea or other, praising us when we got the length of "taking notes" and reading them over on our return; how he would turn the talk ever so naturally to some Bible story or some Martyr reminiscence, or some happy allusion to the "Pilgrim's Progress"! And then it was quite a contest, which of us would get to read aloud, while all the rest listened, and father added here and there a happy thought, or illustration, or anecdote.[44]

The peacemaker will order his home to be a missionary station for lost souls. Lost friends and neighbors will be guests around the dining table. Family prayers will cry out to God to save the unconverted that God sovereignly brings into their lives.

I was a young attorney returning home from a trial in Sacramento, facing twenty-five miles of windshield time on Interstate 5. I remember asking God to give me more opportunities to share my faith. As I entered the on-ramp, there stood a disheveled looking man in his fifties with his thumb stuck out. It was as if God was saying, "Don, here's your opportunity!"

I pulled over, offering a ride as far as the Woodland off-ramp. The man jumped at the offer and hopped in my VW, throwing his bed roll in the back seat. He told me that he was a painter by trade. A life of drunkenness had brought him to abandon his wife. He had been living the homeless life of a hobo, riding the rails across the country for the past ten years. I asked him if he was tired of sleeping under bridges. He told me that he was getting a little old for such a vagabond life. I asked him if he would consider living with Mary and me while I helped him to find painting jobs. With tears in his eyes he answered, "Would you do that for me?"

---

[44] John Payton, *John G. Paton, Missionary to the New Hebrides: An Autobiography, Vol. 2,* Edited by his brother, the Reverend. James Paton, D.D (London, England: Hodder and Stoughton, 1889), 23.

By the way, this predated cell phones, so I couldn't give Mary the heads up before I drove into our driveway. I praise the Lord that God has graced me with a wife who is a peacemaker. Although a little ambivalent, she was onboard with showing this man hospitality. The house ground rules were simple: he was not to be alone in the house with my wife, no smoking or drinking inside, and he would be our guest each Lord's Day at church. God immediately gave him painting jobs, and he remained in our home for a few months.

One Lord's Day, God wonderfully saved this man! During lunch, following his baptism, he told us that he wanted to go back to his wife and be reconciled. He longed for her to experience the same joyful forgiveness with which God had graced him. After ten years of no contact, he wasn't sure whether she had moved on with her life. Nervously, he dialed the only number that he knew. She answered the phone and heard these few words, "I am so sorry. I know the Lord; will you have me back?" There wasn't a dry eye in the Thomas home that day when his wife responded with forgiveness. What a joy it was for me and my wife when we put this man on a bus, headed home to his family to grow in his new life in Christ.

Happy is the home where peacemakers are active in the outreach ministries of their church. This will be the home that delights in distributing Gospel literature and tracts. They will count it a joy to pray for and encourage missionaries serving in other countries. Theirs will not be lives centered on self, but on the eternal well-being of others!

How can you know if a person is a peacemaker? Here are several questions to consider: Do they have a burden for the souls of others? Do they pray for the lost? Do they share their faith with others? Do they give generously to the needs of missionaries? Are they a witness in the community, at work, or at school? Do they personally participate in the outreach ministries of their church?

This Beatitude closes with this glorious blessing: "They shall be called the children of God." Those who have peace with God through faith in Christ and have become peacemakers—faithfully been a conduit of the Gospel to the lost—"They shall be called the children of God." The peacemaker bears the mark of his Heavenly Father, The Peacemaker, who smiles down with Gospel blessings upon His adopted sons.

Marry the peacemaker! "How beautiful are the feet of them that preach the gospel of peace, and bring glad tidings of good things" (Romans 10:15b)! There is one sure way to know if a person is a peacemaker. It is found in the last Beatitude.

Chapter 12

Marry the Persecuted

Blessed are they which are persecuted
for righteousness' sake:
for theirs is the kingdom of heaven.

- Matthew 5:10

As we read in the opening chapter, every fairytale closes with a happy ending. We often read of a giddy couple riding off together on a white steed, silhouetted by a Thomas Kincaid sunset and with turtledoves circling overhead. Even the fuzzy animals of the forest stop and smile with approval as we read the closing words, "And they lived happily ever after. THE END"! So too, as we come to THE END of the Beatitudes, we find our Lord closing with dual promises of happiness and joy!

Each of the Beatitudes is a reminder to us that God's narrow pathway to soul satisfying happiness is not the world's way of trying to achieve the same thing. Hollywood tells us that happiness in marriage is found in two people staring lovingly into each other's eyes. Somehow this happiness continues as they skip off in slow motion, hand-in-hand, through the tulips of life.

As we have been discovering, Jesus rewrote the script in the Beatitudes. Instead of the world's view, we find that true happiness flows from two lives growing in poverty, sadness, meekness, hunger and thirst, mercy, purity and peacemaking. If all of these graces be found in you, there is one last crowning Beatitude that will validate the presence of all the rest—persecution!

When I was attending seminary, students were actually required to take a class in administering and interpreting a written premarital compatibility test. The purpose of this test was to identify and match similar personalities. The premise of the test was that the greater the similarities in personality traits, the greater the compatibility of a couple. This test might sound rational to our psychology driven culture, but it stands in opposition to the Scriptures. Clearly, such testing doesn't fit well within the Old Testament model of arranged marriages. I wonder if Isaac and Rebekah would have passed the test.

The most important marriage test of all is the one that would lead you to marry a true Christian rather than a religious hypocrite. We have been exploring the shorter, eight question test of the Beatitudes. In this chapter, we come to the last question: "Is the person I am considering for marriage persecuted?"

All of the previous Beatitudes which we have seen so far are attitudes or actions which a Christian has or does by the grace of God. He *shows* mercy! He *makes* peace! This last Beatitude is different. This is not something the believer does; it is what others do to all believers who display all of the previous Beatitudes. That's why it might be called the crowning mark of every true Christian. The litmus test of the true Christian is persecution for righteousness' sake. Paul promises, "Yea and all that will live godly in Christ Jesus shall suffer persecution" (2

Timothy 3:12). Paul reminds us that non-Christians
continue to persecute Christians (Galatians 4:29). In fact, it
is ordained by God that you will suffer for His sake
(Philippians 1:29). Martin Luther gave us this short pithy
definition of a Christian: "Christianus Quasi Crucianus" (a
Christian is as if a crucified one).

What does our Lord mean by "persecuted"? The
Greek word here is *"dioko,"* which means to pursue, to
chase away, to harass, to treat with evil, to vex, to molest,
and to pursue to death. The portrait of a Christian is of one
who is earnestly pursued and harassed.

Persecution is inseparable from true faith in Christ.
This is one of the subplots which run throughout the entire
Bible. The history of God's people is a history of
harassment and martyrdom. God has given us the entire
eleventh chapter of Hebrews as a chronological reminder of
the affliction of the faithful saints of the Old Testament.
The first family experienced persecution when Cain slew
his righteous brother Abel (v. 4). Moses chose affliction
rather than the pleasures of Egypt (v. 25). Of the many
unnamed saints in the Old Testament, we sadly read:

> *Women received their dead raised to life again:*
> *and others were tortured, not accepting*
> *deliverance; that they might obtain a better*
> *resurrection: And others had trial of cruel mockings*
> *and scourgings, yea, moreover of bonds and*
> *imprisonment: They were stoned, they were sawn*
> *asunder, were tempted, were slain with the sword:*
> *they wandered about in sheepskins and goatskins;*
> *being destitute, afflicted, tormented; (Of whom the*

world was not worthy:) they wandered in deserts, and in mountains, and in dens and caves of the earth. And these all, having obtained a good report through faith, received not the promise: God having provided some better thing for us, that they without us should not be made perfect (vs. 35-40).

The New Testament opens with John the Baptist having his head served on a platter (Matthew 14:8-10). Our Lord Himself was mocked, beaten and crucified (John 18-19). As Jesus prophesied, every one of the disciples were persecuted, imprisoned, and/or martyred. Tradition tells us that Peter was crucified upside down. Paul the persecutor became Paul the persecuted.

Are they ministers of Christ? (I speak as a fool) I am more; in labours more abundant, in stripes above measure, in prisons more frequent, in deaths oft. Of the Jews five times received I forty stripes save one. Thrice was I beaten with rods, once was I stoned, thrice I suffered shipwreck, a night and a day I have been in the deep; In journeyings often, in perils of waters, in perils of robbers, in perils by mine own countrymen, in perils by the heathen, in perils in the city, in perils in the wilderness, in perils in the sea, in perils among false brethren; In weariness and painfulness, in watchings often, in hunger and thirst, in fastings often, in cold and nakedness (vs. 23-27).

Ignatius tells us that Paul's earthly ministry and suffering came to a tragic end when he was martyred in Rome. The tradition of the church is that he was beheaded under Nero.

Persecution continued against Christians throughout the Roman Empire until Constantine in 313. Nero even went so far as to ignite Christians with fire as living torches. The crowds cheered as lions feasted on believers in the Coliseum. It is believed that during the reign of Diocletian as many as 20,000 Christians were martyred for refusing to offer sacrifices to pagan gods or bow to the emperor as lord.

This history of the persecution of God's people continues to this day. Our faithful Reformers were burned at the stake. In the 1820's, American missionary Adoniram Judson was thrown into a rat-infested Burmese death prison for seventeen months. Missionaries John and Betty Stam were martyred in China in 1934. I recommend that you read some of the Christian classics on persecution like *Foxe's Book of Martyrs,* by John Foxe, *Five English Martyrs*, by J.C. Ryle, and *Through Gates of Splendor*, by Elisabeth Elliot.

You might be thinking at this point, "That was then, and this is the twenty-first century! People are not throwing spears at believers today. We live in a more tolerable time. None of the Christians I know seem persecuted! How can I know if the person I am considering for marriage is persecuted?"

It's true that the church goes through various seasons and degrees of opposition, yet God promises that His people of every age will face persecution. Not all persecution results in martyrdom. We see from Scripture that persecution can be either physical or verbal or both!

What's Inside

The number of ways that men can physically persecute the children of God is only limited by man's fallen imagination. In extreme times, there were whippings, beatings, and imprisonment. Today, in America, it is more common to experience the loss of a job, broken friendships, forfeiture of a promotion, shunning from coworkers, broken family ties and sometimes even broken marriages.

Prior to and during a courtship listen carefully for testimonies of physical persecution. I remember the first time I met a young man who was eager to court one of my daughters. He lived in another state, so I only had a couple of opportunities to visit with him, face to face.

"Tell me a little about yourself," I inquired during one of these opportunities. He told me about his family upbringing and education. He went on to describe his early years of homeschooling as well as his years at the public high school where he excelled both athletically and academically. He was the head of his class and captain of the football team. "When did you graduate?" I asked. I was surprised by his answer.

"I actually didn't."

Having now grabbed my attention, I fired back, "What do you mean, 'actually'?"

He went on to explain why he didn't graduate. Apparently, the local school district had more restrictive graduation requirements than the state. His school required the successful completion of a psychology class. It was this young man's conviction that psychology stood in opposition to biblical truth. He requested an exemption from this requirement or an alternate way he could satisfy their requirement. The principal dug in his heals, proclaiming, "No psychology—no graduation!" He had already completed more than the required number of credits for graduation with a GPA greater than 4.0 in all of his classes. He had also been scheduled to be the valedictorian speaker at his graduation. He appealed to the district school board which affirmed the principal's decision.

This young man chose not to graduate rather than compromise his faith. To encourage his fellow students, he attended the graduation as a guest. His graduation class was so moved by his adherence to his convictions that they all gave him a standing ovation as they entered the auditorium. I was encouraged to meet a young man who understood firsthand his Lord's words, "Blessed are the persecuted."

There is a happy ending to this story. Fast forward a few years. This young man later married my daughter. He went on to graduate from college. My wife recently traveled to be with them for the birth of their second child. Unexpectedly, their phone rang. It was the high school principal on the other end, asking for forgiveness for what had taken place in the past. He surprisingly invited my son-in-law to come down to his office and graduate from high school. The school district had saved his diploma all of those years. My daughter, their children, and my wife proudly watched as he marched down the aisle of the principal's office to receive his diploma.

Physical persecutions are rare in our culture today. Jesus reminds us of the more common, verbal form of persecution, "Blessed (happy) are ye, when men shall revile you..." (Matthew 5:11a). Reviling is mocking someone to his face. The onlookers mocked Jesus on the Cross: "And they that passed by railed on him, wagging their heads, and saying, Ah, thou that destroyest the temple, and buildest it in three days, Save thyself, and come down from the cross. Likewise also the chief priests mocking said among themselves with the scribes, He saved others; himself he cannot save" (Mark 15:29-31).

During courtship, listen for words that might describe being reviled. You might ask the person if they have ever been persecuted for their faith. If not, whether they have ever taken a stand in opposition to the world for Christ? Those who walk a committed walk are often mocked as "Bible thumpers! Legalists! Holy Rollers! Holier than thou!" One of my son Stephen's first jobs was working on an out-of-town construction project. When he wouldn't join in the swearing and drinking at night, he earned the new name, "Moses." For the rest of the job it was "Hey, Moses!" What they meant as mocking, he took as a badge of joy.

Another way enemies of the Gospel verbally persecute is when they "say all manner of evil against you falsely, for my name's sake" (verse 11b). This includes slander and all other forms of false accusations that go to a person's character. Jesus was falsely accused of being the devil incarnate (John 8:48)! The big thinkers of the day mocked Paul on Mars Hill as he preached the resurrection (Acts 17:32). So too, the promise today to all who are in Christ is that they also will be mocked and reviled.

One of the things I have noticed during my personal

Christian journey is that my skin has increasingly grown thicker. Perhaps this is part of God's sanctifying work in my life. There was a time, as a young Christian, that the slightest verbal jab ripped me apart. It hurt to be called a "Bible thumper." Over the years the attacks have intensified. I have been reviled as have my wife and children. I now count this a joy.

If you embrace a life of holiness and are swimming upstream from the current of the world, be prepared to be labeled a "legalist." If you hold to a biblically ordered family, in which the husband lovingly leads his wife and the wife lovingly submits to her husband's headship, be prepared to be charged with "spousal abuse." If you are committed to serving as a member of a biblically ordered church, you might be labeled as a "cultist." Nothing is off limits when it comes to persecution. You will be attacked in every area of the Christian life.

We need to be careful to note what our Lord **is not** saying, as well as what He **is** saying, if we are going to properly understand and apply this Beatitude. Jesus is not saying, "Blessed are those who face painful hardships because of their own lack of due diligence." You can't self-righteously claim persecution because you were fired for your poor work ethic. Neither does Jesus say, "Blessed are those who are persecuted for their religious fanaticism." When you are mocked for waving "Thank God for Dead Soldiers" or "Pray More for Dead Soldiers" posters at the funeral of a fallen warrior, don't think for a minute that God is gracing you with blessings.

Jesus is very explicit when He said, "Blessed are

they which are persecuted *for righteousness' sake."* In other words, this is true because of, or on account of, God's righteousness brightly shining through you. Blessed are those who are persecuted for being Christ-like! Christians will be persecuted for their lives of holiness. Jesus told Nicodemus that those whose hearts are evil hate the light (John 3:20-21).

A life that shines brightly with the light of integrity exposes, convicts, and provokes anger in sinners around them. This is the very anger that drove the multitudes of Jews to cry out against Jesus, "Crucify Him! Crucify Him!" Sin and righteousness are natural enemies, just like dogs and cats. Those who are striving to work their way to God's favor hate the Gospel of grace! Those whose lives are in turmoil hate those who experience the peace and joy of knowing Christ!

I learned very early in my Christian life that unbelievers who wallow in their sins reject and revile those who are turning from and mourning over their sins. God graciously saved me during my last year in law school. There was a group of us that lived in the western Chicago suburbs who rode the train every day to class. After the last class on Friday, we would frequent the bar in the train station in search of some *liquid* joy. The Friday following my conversion, I sat down with the guys and shared with them my new faith in Jesus Christ. I told them that God had changed me! "I am now a new creature in Christ!" I still wanted to be their friend and get together with them on Fridays, but I just wouldn't be drinking any more. That was it! That's all they needed to hear. Our "friendship" was suddenly over. I had wrongfully thought that my drinking buddies were my true friends. What I discovered was that it was only our sin that we had in common! Once the sin was removed, the friendship was gone.

Do you see why this is the crowning mark of all the Beatitudes? If you are living out the first seven Beatitudes before the eyes of an unbelieving world, that world will lash out at you with the persecution of the eighth.

How can you know if the person you are considering to marry is persecuted? Watch his life and listen to his words. This is a fertile area of discussion for courtship conversation. Some evening or Sunday afternoon you might open your Bibles together and read a passage like those included in this chapter and discuss the persecution of today. You might ask questions like:

- "Was there ever a time in your life when you experienced this kind of persecution? If not, why not?"

- "Do you think you can be a Christian and never experience any form of persecution?"

- "What would it take to precipitate this kind of physical or verbal harassment today?"

Why is it so important that you marry the persecuted? As we have already seen, it is one of the marks of every true Christian. It's the one litmus test that helps separate the hypocrite from the holy. It may well be that the person you are considering for courtship has not yet experienced persecution in their Christian walk. Then ask yourself, "Is this person living a zealous life that confronts a sinful world with the grace of God?" Are they living a life that will one day lead to persecution? The false professing Christian who is swimming downstream in the currents of worldliness will never experience the pain of persecution for righteousness' sake.

Also, persecution is the sure path to happiness and blessing in marriage. Happy are the persecuted? Yes! It strikes us as counter intuitive, doesn't it? How can a life of beatings, harassment, reviling, mocking, and even martyrdom bring happiness and blessing? God's economy is not man's economy. Here are several ways in which the heavy hand of persecution can bring happiness, not only to your life, but the life of your family.

Persecution produces in the heart of every true believer the fruit of happiness that comes from a full assurance of salvation! To the persecuted, Jesus promises the blessing of the kingdom of heaven (v. 10). Theirs (and theirs alone) is (present tense) the Kingdom of God. In other words, persecution for righteousness' sake is the evidence that you are a citizen of God's kingdom. That's why Peter encourages the believers who have scattered due to persecution, "Beloved, think it not strange concerning the fiery trial which is to try you, as though some strange thing happened unto you: But rejoice, inasmuch as ye are partakers of Christ's sufferings; that, when his glory shall be revealed, ye may be glad also with exceeding joy" (1 Peter 4:12-13).

Jesus is your king! You are His subject! You have all the blessings as a citizen, and all of these blessings will infinitely intensify in the eternal state. Can there be any greater happiness than to belong to the King of Creation?

The cost of this discipleship is to live a life of persecution or even martyrdom. What greater happiness can there be than to follow in our King's footsteps of sacrifice and pick up your cross to follow Him?

That's why this is the only Beatitude that carries with it the dual commands to "Rejoice, and be exceeding glad..." (v. 12). "Rejoice" from the Greek *"chairo"* means to be full of cheer, to enjoy a state of happiness. It is not so much an emotion as it is an attitude and fruit of the Spirit (Galatians 5:22-23). To this, Christ adds the command to be exceedingly glad, which literally carries the meaning of "jumping for joy"! This joy is not some painted-on smile; it is the joy that springs up from within, causing the whole body to leap for joy!

Richard Wurmbrand, pastor and founder of Voice of the Martyrs Ministries, writes of this joy in his book, *Tortured for Christ*. When ordered to stop preaching by the Romanian dictator, he chose to obey Christ rather than man. He was released in 1956 after serving an eight and one-half year prison sentence for faithfully continuing to preach the Gospel.

Warned not to do so again, he continued to preach Christ. He was rearrested in 1959 and imprisoned a second time, for twenty-five years. Such torture for righteousness' sake might still be rare in the western world, but it is rapidly on the increase in Islamic countries. What was Wurmbrand's response to his isolation and mistreatment? He experienced joy, literally to the point of rising up in his weakness and dancing around his cell, confident that angels were dancing with him! Upon release he went home to his wife, Sabina, and they fasted and prayed as a memorial to the joy which he had experienced in the face of the horrors of prison.

There is also happiness in knowing that persecution is God's means for purifying His people. Thomas Watson pithily adds, "Suffering times are sifting times."[45] Peter strengthens the joy of the suffering saints of Asia Minor with the promise that their suffering will be God's very means to perfect, strengthen and establish them in their faith (1 Peter 5:10). What greater happiness could there be than knowing that through the enemies' sword of persecution God is making you and your family more and more like the Lord Jesus Christ?

There is also a blessing that passes to the children of persecuted parents. Where parents are being harassed, ridiculed, and slandered for righteousness' sake, their children grow up in an arena of a costly faith lived out before their eyes. The suffering of our Savior will be seen through the suffering of the family. These are children who learn at an early age the difference between hypocrisy and true discipleship.

The godly John Rogers was sentenced to death under Bloody Mary for his opposition to the false teachings of the Church of Rome. His pardon would be signed, if only Rogers would recant. To do so would be to deny his Lord. He was burned at the stake on February 4, 1555. His wife and eleven children escorted him to the place of burning to encourage their husband and father. The French ambassador, Noailles, describes the tender scene, "Even his

---

[45] Thomas Watson, *The Beatitudes,* 262.

children assisted at it, comforting him in such a manner that it seemed as if he had been led to a wedding."[46] Surely the fiery loss of their father emblazed in their hearts a faith-producing understanding of the cost of true discipleship.

How can death and martyrdom produce happiness in the Christian home? The first question of the Westminster Shorter Catechism asks, "What is the chief end of man?" to which it rightly answers, "Man's chief end is to glorify God, and to enjoy him forever" (1 Corinthians 10:31). This tells us that the one chief end of a Christian marriage is to glorify God and enjoy Him forever. Surely the greatest joy comes from glorifying God through your greatest sacrifice, the offering of your reputation and your very life for Christ's sake.

This was the heartfelt passion of John and Betty Stam, missionaries to China in 1934. God had blessed them with a three-month old daughter. The country was being overrun by atheistic Chinese communist soldiers. The couple was imprisoned. From jail, John wrote, "Philippians 1:20: 'May Christ be glorified whether by life or death.'" God answered his prayer by way of the sword on a hillside much like the one our Savior was crucified on.

John had turned to the leader of the band, asking mercy for this man. When he was sharply ordered to kneel—and the look of joy on his face, afterwards, told of the unseen Presence with them as his spirit was released—Betty was seen to quiver,

---

[46] Joseph Chester, *John Rogers: The Compiler of the First Authorized English Bible* (London: Longman, Green, Longman and Roberts, 1861), 152.

but only for a moment. Bound as she was, she fell on her knees beside him. A quick command, the flash of a sword which mercifully she did not see—and they were reunited.[47]

God chose to graciously spare the life of their daughter, little baby Helen. In death, this dear couple continues to glorify God through their gravestones in China:

Elizabeth Scott Stam

February 22, 1906

"For me to live is Christ

And to die is gain" Phil. 1:21.

John Cornelius Stam

January 18, 1907

"That Christ may be magnified

whether by life or by death" Phil. 1:20.

Marry the persecuted. This is the marriage where couples truly live, happily ever after, "for great is your reward in heaven" (v. 12).

---

[47] Mrs. Taylor, Howard, *John and Betty Stam: A Story of Triumph* (Chicago: Moody Press, 1982), 119-120.

Chapter 13

Where Are They?

Whoso findeth a wife findeth a good thing,
and obtaineth favour of the Lord.

- Proverbs 18:22

Who can find a virtuous woman?
for her price is far above rubies.

- Proverbs 31:10

Behind our house in rural Wyoming is a huge anthill that forms a one-foot high dome that houses a mega-colony of industrious red ants. Several years ago, the geology leader for our local 4-H Club took one of my sons on a field trip that included one of these giant ant hills. Why an ant hill? The kids were told that there was a rich cache of gemstones hidden underground. As the strong ants tunnel their way deeper into the earth, they sometimes deposit sand on the surface, occasionally mixed with garnets and even tiny blood red rubies! That's all the kids needed to hear as they dropped to their knees and franticly began sifting through the huge mound of biting ants in search of their own sparkling gems. My son and I looked carefully through the bag of interesting rocks he had brought home that day, but we found no rubies!

The ruby's strikingly beautiful red color, combined with its rarity, make it as valuable today as it was in Old Testament times. Actress Elizabeth Taylor's 8.24 carat ruby ring was recently auctioned by Christie's for over $4.2 million! You can crawl on your knees from one Wyoming ant hill to another, sifting through ton after ton of tiny chips of worthless rocks and never find a precious ruby. Still, I must confess, every time I walk by our ant hill, I stop and carefully gaze, hoping I might see a little red stone sparkling in the sand.

The Scriptures remind us that a godly husband and wife are as rare and valuable as a ruby. The Proverbs ask, "Who can find a virtuous woman? for her price *is* far above rubies" (Proverbs 31:10). The person that God would have you marry is a rare find. People are as numerous as the sands on the beach, but a godly man or woman is as precious and beautiful as a ruby.

For all who desire to discover a godly person to marry, this raises a whole host of important and highly practical questions. Where do you find these rubies? How do you mine the rare beauty of godliness? What do you do when there are no godly single men or women in your church? What if you find yourself in your thirties or forties and still have not found that hidden gem of a spouse? Do you continue your pursuit of the priceless ruby or do you begin your search for a rhinestone? Do you stay where you are and continue what you have been doing until God brings the right person to you, or should you become a spiritual prospector who franticly embarks on a life-long quest for that rare gem of a spouse?

The answers to these questions are rooted in the deeper theological questions that fall into one of two extremes. Has God sovereignly predetermined whom you are to marry, leaving you to passively wait until he brings you Mr. or Mrs. Right? Or is God detached, and has He left the discovery of your ruby totally up to your freewill and ability?

Since my first child approached the age of courtship, God has helped me see a more balanced approach to discovering His will in marriage. In my early days of parenting, I knew that God was sovereign over all things, including marriage, so my counsel swung in the more extreme direction of sovereignty at the expense of personal responsibility. My counsel to my children was to "be the person that God wants you to be, where He wants you to be, and He will providentially drop the person you are to marry right into midst of your life."

In support of my advice, I would tell the story of the missionary family our church supported in Papua, New Guinea. When their son turned eighteen, he was faced with the choice of returning to the United States to pursue his education and a wife or remain in New Guinea working with the tribal people whom he dearly loved. He was perplexed and didn't know what to do. On the one hand, he strongly wanted to be married; on the other hand, he believed that God was calling him to minister to the tribal people he had grown up with. He was convinced that there were no marriageable young ladies in the remote jungle where he lived. What did he do? He chose to forgo his pursuit of marriage and to remain faithful to his calling in New Guinea. This meant a life of singleness. God had a different plan. A few years later, the missionary board that sent him decided to open a regional mission station a short distance from where he was living. Amazingly, they sent a beautiful young lady to oversee this new office. By the providence of God, the two were married shortly thereafter!

For many others, the pendulum swings away from sovereignty to the extreme of self-determination. Here you will find single Christians franticly digging through one anthill of life after another in search of that rare ruby. They will do anything to find Mr. or Mrs. Right. They will frequently transfer from job to job, move from state to state, and migrate from church to church. For them, the biological clock is ticking, and it is up to them to find the right person to marry before it is too late.

While I was attending seminary, one of our young, single members of our church family—who had just graduated from college—moved in with our family. She was an attractive young lady, but more importantly, she passionately loved the Lord and desired marriage over a career. At the time, I was pastoring a small inner-city church with a greying membership. This young woman loved the church, but she also wanted to be married. One day, she came to me and sadly told me that she would be leaving our church to attend a huge mega-church in another city. She reasoned that our church had no single men and her new church had a large singles ministry with several hundred people. We wished her well and continued to pray that God would grace her with a husband.

She faithfully attended all of the singles gatherings at her new mega-church for over a year without one young man asking her out on a date. She also knew that I was attending seminary with classrooms full of young men who longed to study the Word and serve the Lord. I'll never forget the day she told me that she had enrolled in a seminary class. Although she knew that God calls men to the Gospel ministry, she reasoned that she could benefit from an Mrs. degree over a M. Div. (Masters of Divinity). Sadly, she left the seminary without a single date.

The spiritual irony of her journey was that, shortly thereafter, God did sovereignly bring her current husband into her life. But He did so in His own way. One afternoon, while helping a girlfriend paint her house, a man walked up who would later become her husband. She was dressed in overalls, paint covered her face, and her hair was tied up in a bandana at the time. God brought them together in spite of her best efforts, leaving God to get all of the glory!

I have come to what I believe to be a more biblically balanced pathway to discovering the person you are to marry. Yes, God is sovereign. He has decreed all things, including the person you are to marry (or not), before the foundations of the world had been laid! But we also see in Scripture that God has ordained the means through which He exercises His will.

Under the Old Covenant, the ordinary means were simple: dad arranged the marriage. One of the most graphic examples of parental arrangement was the marriage of Isaac to Rebekah. With no suitable wives amongst the Canaanites, Abraham sent his servant, Eliezer, to find a wife for Isaac in the land of his people (Genesis 24). Rebekah passed the man-made test of watering his camels, causing the servant to choose Rebekah as God's will for Isaac. This choice was affirmed when her father added his approval. After Rebekah gave her consent, gifts were bestowed upon her and her father, and Rebekah was caravanned off to Canaan to marry Isaac. Such arranged marriages were never prescribed by Scripture. They grew out of God-given paternal authority and were later adopted by many other cultures and religious traditions. Although Christian fathers today still retain their God-given role of oversight of their daughter's courtship, the means of finding that precious jewel of a spouse have changed with the culture.

The first means for finding the person you are to marry is to commit the matter to prayer. James directs all who lack wisdom to call on God, who delights in abundantly supplying His wisdom (James 1:5). There are few areas of our Christian life where you need more wisdom than that of discerning the person you are to marry. It takes wisdom to know God's criteria for a godly spouse. It requires God-given discernment to know the person's spiritual heart along with the presence of mutual compatibility. When Eliezer sought wisdom in knowing God's will for Isaac, he prayed, "O LORD God of my master Abraham, I pray thee, send me good speed this day, and shew kindness unto my master Abraham" (Genesis 24:12). Faithfully pray that God will lead you to the person He would have you marry.

Others should be sought to intercede on your behalf. Parents should begin praying when their children are still very young for God's provision of their future spouses. I can remember sharing with our children when they were very young that, if it be God's will, they too would one day marry like Mom and Dad did. I routinely told our young daughters that the man that they would one day marry was at that very moment with his family somewhere in the world. Then we would bow our heads and pray that God would one day bring them together at His divine time and place.

These intercessory prayers should expand to your church family. There seems to be a self-imposed stigma on being single today. Single people are often reluctant to let others know their desire to be married. It's a good thing to desire marriage! Our churches cry out to God for the salvation of lost friends and loved ones. We request that the body of Christ plea before the throne of grace for our jobs, housing, physical healing, and spiritual trials. But what about marriage?

Several years ago, one of the young men in our college ministry had a strong desire to marry. He longed for a precious ruby. Every time the church gathered to pray, he would request prayers for a wife. I remember several prayer meetings when he could be heard pleading with God, "Father, I will take the bottom of the barrel, if you will bless me with a wife." God wonderfully answered his prayers, as He often does, beyond his expectations and gave him, not the barrel's bottom, but the rare precious cream of a godly wife that rose to the top of the barrel.

Pray for one another that God sends godly husbands and wives to them! Dads, ask the church to pray for spouses for your children. Elders, encourage the flock to share their prayer requests for godly husbands and wives. Young, single people, let your requests be known to your church if it is your desire to marry. Ask the brethren to intercede on your behalf that God might grace you with wisdom and heavenly guidance.

Secondly, be proactive by faithfully gathering where other serious minded believers gather. God is sovereign, but these opportunities are often the very means that God uses to bring a couple together. If your heart is passionate about missions, enlist for short-term missionary service. In 2010 a 7.0 earthquake rocked Haiti, killing more than 300,000 people and leaving one million homeless. A team of relief workers was sent from our church to Port-au-Prince. They met Julie, a single nurse, who had come to minister from another state. Her plan was to return home after a short missionary trip. God's plan was different. Amazingly, she stayed to care for the suffering people and later met and married a Haitian pastor!

Dads, if your travels take you to other churches, consider taking your sons or daughters along with you. A few years ago, I received a phone call from a pastor in another rural state more than a thousand miles away. Towards the end of the conversation, he abruptly inquired, "By the way, do you have any godly singles in your church? We have several precious sons and daughters, but there are very few marriageable young people in our church or community." I told him that we had several singles that would make wonderful husbands and wives. Apparently, he shared my report with some of his church members. A year later, one of his church families with eleven children decided to make our little corner of Wyoming their vacation destination. I have fond memories of making new friends and enjoying their fellowship. Several years later, the same family decided on a return vacation to Wyoming. By now, their younger children were in their teens. This time, more lasting relationships were made, including the one between my daughter and one of their sons, who found his precious ruby in Wyoming.

Consider attending Bible conferences where serious-minded single people will be present. This might require some advanced planning and savings. For several years, our church sponsored an annual singles conference. Young believers from across the country and abroad gathered for four days of Bible preaching and social opportunities to make new friends. Over the years, several of these couples have joined their hearts to become one flesh in the bond of Christian love.

Finally, there is a third ordinary means that is no longer that ordinary. In fact, it's a means you might think to be a little old fashioned. I introduce you to the important role of "matchmaking" in discovering the person that God would have you marry. Even its name carries a negative connotation, filled with meddling, scheming and abuse. Perhaps you think of images of Yente, the village matchmaker in "Fiddler on the Roof," who tells Golde that a rich widower by the name of Lazar Wolf wants to marry her daughter, Tzeitel. It was Jewish tradition that this young girl, from a poor family, must marry whatever husband the matchmaker brings, rather than the young man of her own choosing. Tzeitel laments with these opening lyrics:

Make me a match,
Find me a find,
catch me a catch
Matchmaker, Matchmaker

What's Inside

Look through your book,
And make me a perfect match.

It is time that we take a closer look at matchmaking and rediscover it's biblical roots. Perhaps it is time to give it a makeover and even a name change. Let's begin by first defining our term, "matchmaker." A matchmaker is any mature believer who aids in the bringing together of two single Christians for the purpose of pursuing God's will in marriage. Notice that it is important that the matchmaker be a mature Christian. Matchmaking should not be based on outward criteria or even common areas of interest, but rather on the inward character of the heart. He should be a person who can discern in others the presence of the fruit of salvation, who knows the marks of loving leadership in a man and godly submission in the woman's heart.

There are several examples of matchmaking in the Bible. The first can be found in the opening pages of Genesis. God, the perfect matchmaker, created Adam and made Eve to be his wife. He brought them together, and they were perfectly suited for each other (Genesis 2:18-24). As we have already seen, Abraham asked Eliezer, his trusted servant, to be a matchmaker for his son Isaac (Genesis 24). He found a young lady named Rebekah who met the criteria Abraham had given, and Isaac loved Rebekah and married her. We see Naomi taking on the role of matchmaker as she instructs her widowed daughter-in-law to go and lie at the feet of Boaz while he sleeps and to wait for him to tell her what to do (Ruth 3:4).

A matchmaker can be a friend that invites a couple for dinner. This happened in our family while I was attending seminary and teaching at a nearby Christian law school. One of my students had a strong desire to marry. He shared with me that he did not trust himself to go out and find a potential wife and get to know her through the dating process. It was his conviction that he would first be introduced to the person he would marry by a faithful matchmaker who had first seen godly qualities in each of their lives. I remember thinking at the time that this seemed like a very strange approach. Mary and I knew a young lady in Bible College that seemed to us to be a good match, and we invited them both over to our house for Mary's supreme spaghetti dinner! I don't know where the relationship went from there, but I felt I had been faithful in my role of a matchmaker.

I also want to encourage pastors and church elders to consider matchmaking as part of their shepherding role of the flock of God. There are young single ladies and single men in smaller churches and communities who desire to marry, but there are few singles for them to consider for marriage. Not only should we be praying for godly singles in our churches, we should be active in letting other pastors become aware of them.

We see this pastoral matchmaking in the life of John Calvin. It was matchmaker, Martin Bucer, a fellow reformer in Strasbourg who, a few months after Calvin's arrival, found a prospective spouse for Calvin to consider. There is no evidence that Calvin had ever met her. Nothing ever came of this courtship. Within three months, another matchmaker, pastor and reformer, William Farel, found another woman for Calvin. John Witte Jr. adds, "Farel apparently had asked Calvin what he was looking for in a mate. Calvin blurted out the requisite qualifications bluntly. 'I am not one of those insane kinds of lovers who, once smitten by the first sight of a fine figure, cherishes even the faults of his lover. The only beauty that seduces me is of one who is chaste, not too fastidious, modest, thrifty, patient, and hopefully she will be attentive to my health.'"[48] With such a laundry list of expectations, one should not be surprised that this woman also quickly disappeared.

Calvin himself took on the role of matchmaker. Witt continues, "Most of his matchmaking efforts—though not all—were privately pursued on behalf of well-connected friends and patrons, particularly fellow ministers."[49] One of his more notable efforts is illustrated by his search for a wife for the widower, fellow pastor and close friend, Pierre Viret. Calvin's early inquiries seemed to produce no results. There were many women, but no apparent rubies. Finally, his labors were blessed by God, and he later joyfully wrote to Viret, "The more we inquire, the more numerous and the better are the testimonies with which the young lady is honored."[50] All of Calvin's efforts proved in vain when her father rejected the idea of her moving to Geneva and refused to give his daughter's hand in marriage. Viret later found his own wife without the help of a matchmaker.

Pastors might consider including in their correspondences with like-minded sister churches a note of introduction to some of the singles in their churches. I

---

[48] John Witte Jr. and Robert M. Kingdon, *Sex, Marriage, and Family in John Calvin's Geneva – Courtship, Engagement, and Marriage,* 98.

[49] Ibid., 100.

[50] Ibid., 102.

know of one pastor who had one of his single young ladies fill out a biographical questionnaire, complete with her areas of interest and testimony that he sent out to other churches. He encouraged the pastors to give a copy to any godly young men they might recommend. If interested, these young men would contact the young lady's father who would determine how to proceed. Several men responded and the father gave one his permission to come and meet his daughter face to face.

There is a new matchmaker out there that has found its way into our twenty-fist century culture, more properly known as the Internet dating site. Millions of young Christian singles have uploaded their profiles and pictures with a prayer that it might be sovereignly linked with "Mr. or Mrs. Right." These Internet dating sites come with their strengths as well as dangers. The biggest strength is that your profile can be seen by a multitude of others online. I know several married couples who were introduced by one of these Internet matchmakers and seem to be happily married. However, be warned, there are many more that were deceived or victimized through the Internet.

The Internet is filled with snares. One of our church elders recently retired as our local chief of police. His training included FBI classes in policing Internet predators. We both responded to a call for help from a husband in our church whose wife had become involved with a man in India over the Internet. She was about to leave her husband and two children to live out her twisted fantasy in India. Our elder turned to her and said, "Tell me one verifiable fact that you know to be true about this man."

She paused and thought through his challenge. "Well," she replied, reaching for a tiny photograph next to her computer, "I have this picture." She showed us a picture of what appeared to be an Indian man in his mid-thirties.

This elder challenged her further, "How do you know that this is the man that you have been communicating with?" He went on to explain that frequently nothing is what it appears on the Internet, warning her that she might have even been corresponding with a predator, minor child, married man, or even another woman! Sadly, this marriage ended on a tragic note when she sinfully chose to exchange her dear family for an unverified, online fantasy.

If you choose to use one of the Christian dating sites to be your matchmaker, be careful, prayerful, and wise. One of the great dangers of this service is that it is impossible to know a person's heart over the Internet. To truly know someone's heart, you must have a face to face relationship in which you can observe their walk and listen to their talk. It's important that you converse with others who know them as well. An invaluable wealth of background information can be learned by visiting first hand with pastors, friends, and relatives.

Here are a few practical cautions for you to consider:

- **Careful selection.** There are many sites that differ in their approach. Several of the larger websites are secular sites whose searches can be filtered by religious categories. Beware of the danger of becoming emotionally involved with someone who is not saved. One of the more popular sites requires a personality test which they use to match couples by their compatibility. You should ask yourself if compatibility testing is God's means of discerning whom you should marry. There are other sites that target exclusively professing Christians (in the broadest sense of the term). These often screen for compatibility through questionnaires about doctrinal beliefs and personal lifestyle convictions. You should consider dating sites that limit their members to those who hold similar doctrinal or denominational distinctives.

- **Parental involvement.** I would encourage Christian singles to involve their parents in the matchmaking process. You must be careful that you don't set up a secret virtual reality outside the realm of parental oversight. Ask for your father's guidance in responding to Internet inquiries. Share your passwords with your parents. Young ladies, consider using your father's email address. Let him be the contact person. He can best ask the hard questions and do the initial detective work before he gives the green light to proceed on his terms. If there are any red flags, it is much easier for dad to be the one who says "no" and breaks off communication.

- **Good detective work.** Discerning the heart of a person online requires extra scrutiny. A father should not hesitate to do a complete background check. If churches require such checks for Sunday school teachers and nursery attendants, how much more should a father require one of a person who comes calling online? Don't be afraid to ask hard questions about prior marriages, arrests, and financial credit. Request and follow up on references from employers, schools, and especially their church pastor. Any person pursuing one of your children should be an active, serving member of a local church.

- **Public meetings.** Always take a friend, family member, or preferably your father when meeting a person for the first time. Realistically, they are little more than a stranger to you. Make sure your meeting is in a visible, public setting. Never allow them to drive you somewhere or take you where you will be alone.

- **Wisdom and precaution.** Remember that things are not always what they appear. Use the wisdom that comes from above, marked by prayerful precaution as you seek God's will.

If all you want is gravel, a quick call to your local sand and rock vendor will bring to your front yard one ton of gravel for about $10.00! Gravel is both abundant and cheap. But if it's a sparkling, blood-red ruby that you are looking for, you will have to search both far and wide. Such a precious stone is not only rare, but valuable. For a five-carat gem that is dark red and perfectly clear, expect to pay in excess of $25,000. The Scriptures are a reminder that a godly spouse is even *more* rare and valuable than a ruby. Don't settle for spiritual gravel. It is true that God is sovereign over whom you will, or even *if* you will, marry. It is also true that we are to actively prospect for that precious jewel through the ordinary means He has given us.

In summary, remember, to bring your desire for marriage before the throne of grace. Ask God to bring a godly person into your life as well as the wisdom to discern His will. Secondly, be willing to step out of your daily routine and gather where other serious minded believers gather. Finally, consider the godly counsel of others. Leave open the option of God using a matchmaker to introduce you to the person you are to marry.

You might ask, "What if, after faithfully availing myself of all of God's ordinary means, I still remain single? What do I do now?"

Chapter 14

Happy Are the Single!

But I want you to be free from concern. One who is unmarried is concerned about the things of the Lord, how he may please the Lord;

- 1 Corinthians 7:32 NASB

Our culture has been molded into the mindset that true happiness can only be found in marriage. It's a message that comes to us early. During a young girl's first trip through Fantasyland, Cinderella, Snow White, and Sleeping Beauty all become life-sized lessons of how true, everlasting happiness comes from being married to a handsome prince. This ongoing pressure to marry is both subtle and blatant.

The princess fantasy continues to be reinforced by parents, peers, magazines, Hollywood, and yes, even the church. As you get older, you begin to hear subtle, and sometimes not so subtle, jokes and jabs asking, "When are you going to find Mr. or Mrs. Right?" This push towards marriage can be so great that many are brought to feel that their ongoing singleness amounts to a failed life. Even the thought of living a single life fosters the grim fear of becoming an old maid, lonely hermit—a pariah. You cannot truly know the will of God in marriage unless you first stop and consider whether His will might include a life of singleness.

Fairytales are just that—fairytales. We are not living in the Magic Kingdom of Disney, but the glorious Kingdom of God! The apostle Paul commands us to not be pressured and shaped by this world's system, but rather be transformed by the renewing of your mind (Romans 12:2). You can only live this transformed life if you are willing to first submit to the apostle Paul's appeal to sacrificially present your body and very self to God (v. 1).

You cannot separate your marital state from your spiritual state. Many young Christians are blinded to God's will about the single life because they are too self-focused rather than God-focused. Often, the question of marriage is driven by, "What will make me happy? What will let me best keep 'my' life-agenda?" This obsession becomes, "my" wedding, "my" dress, "my" guests, "my" honeymoon, "my" children, and "my" house with its white picket fence. It is a life driven by me, me, me!

We have come to see that the transformed life is not about you; it is about Jesus Christ! It is a heartfelt dethroning of self and movement towards a radical life of discipleship. If you are truly trusting in Jesus as your Savior, you have denied yourself and picked up your cross of sacrifice to follow Him daily as your Lord. He's given you a new heart with a passion to worship and serve. It is a heart that beats with mercy and compassion for the lost and hurting people all around you. It is a heart that delights in serving your brothers and sisters in Christ.

Jesus sounds the alarm that time is short. Paul exhorts you to redeem the time. There is so much to do and so little time in which to do it. You only have one brief opportunity to serve and glorify God this side of eternity. How are you going to best spend it? You might be asking, "What does the cost of discipleship have to do with whether I marry or remain single?" Simply this: before you can know God's will regarding your marital status, you must ask yourself, "In what state can I best fulfill His calling for my life?"

Remember, God created marriage. Marriage is good. This covenant relationship was God's ordained means for overcoming loneliness (Genesis 2:18), providing companionship (Genesis 2:18), procreation (Genesis 1:28), intimate enjoyment (Hebrews 12:4), as well as displaying to the world a living picture of Christ's love for His church (Ephesians 5:22-33). However, marriage was never intended to be His exclusive will for every Christian. In fact, as we are going to see, the single life can be both a gift and blessing of God.

In 1 Corinthians 7, Paul spends the entire chapter answering questions about matters relating to marriage. More than one-half of the chapter (vs. 26-40) is given over to Paul addressing questions from the Corinthians believers relating to the single, unmarried life. (You won't find the same balance on Amazon or in your local Christian bookstore!) There are blessings that come with being single, but the most important to note is that being single is a calling *and* a gift.

Paul first introduces the high calling of the single life as one of God's gifts. If it were left to him, Paul wishes that everyone could share the same single state that he apparently experienced (v. 8). However, he adds that not everyone has been blessed with the same gifting from God. God's will for many is a life of marriage while He gifts others to be single. Virginity is a special enabling of God whereby He frees all who are so gifted for kingdom service. Jesus taught that "there are some eunuchs, which were so born from *their* mother's womb: and there are some eunuchs, which were made eunuchs of men: and there be eunuchs, which have made themselves eunuchs for the kingdom of heaven's sake. He that is able to receive *it*, let him receive *it*" (Matthew 19:12).

Not only is the single life a gift from God, it is a good gift. Later in the seventh chapter of 1 Corinthians, Paul addresses the question of whether unmarried virgin daughters should enter into the covenant of marriage. Although it was lawful for them to marry, it was not advisable for them to do so in light of the present distress that they faced (v. 26). The same God that declares that it is not good for a man to live alone now balances that teaching by expressing that it is also good to be single. Although this teaching is not directly from the words of Christ, the writing of Paul in 1 Corinthians is the inspired Word of God and is authoritative in your life. It is not a matter of whether marriage is better than the single life; they are both good. The real question is: in what state would God call you to best glorify Him in your life?

You might be wondering, "How can I glorify God by remaining single?" Paul lists 4 ways the single life brings glory to God and brings good to you and those around you:

#1 – It Is the Best Way to Endure Persecution

Paul reasons that the single life is the best life in light of the "present distress" (v. 26). This "present distress" was Paul's way of describing a great persecution that the church was experiencing under the iron hand of the Roman Empire. Paul was subjected to persecution as he faced riots, beatings, and imprisonment. Just a decade after writing this letter, Nero began a persecution that resulted in the arrest, beating and torture of many believers. In 64 AD a great fire broke out, burning down much of Rome. Many historians believe that Nero started the fire and made the Christians his scapegoat.

Married life would have made such tumultuous times even more difficult. Imagine how the Apostle Paul's ministry would have been different if he had been married. Imagine Paul trying to support a wife and children as he traveled from city to city preaching the Cross. As a single man, he had great liberty to go and suffer on behalf of Christ.

Paul is not saying that married couples cannot go to the mission field and raise a family. He is not even saying that married couples should not face Christian persecution together. The history of the church is full of such sacrificial examples. Many faithful couples have walked hand in hand through the fires of persecution and martyrdom.

Back in the nineteenth century, the New Hebrides, a 450 mile chain of islands in the South Pacific that now form the Republic of Vanuatu, was inhabited by cannibals. The first two pioneer missionaries were killed and eaten shortly after making shore. Several years later, in 1859,

John G. Paton married Mary Ann Robson. Fourteen days later, the couple set sail from London to take the Gospel to the tribal people of the New Hebrides. Mary was pregnant by the time the young newlyweds landed on the island of Tanna. Nineteen days after giving birth to young Peter, just three months after arriving in the New Hebrides, Mary died from a tropical fever. Then, precious Peter became ill and died at only 36 days old.

Paton sadly recounts, "The ever-merciful Lord sustained me, to lay the precious dust of my beloved ones in the same quiet grave, dug for them close by at the end of the house; in all of which last offices my own hands, despite breaking heart, had to take the principal share! I built the grave round and round with coral blocks, and covered the top with beautiful white coral, broken small as graves; and the spot became my sacred and much-frequented shrine, during the following months and years when I laboured on for the salvation of these savage Islanders amidst difficulties, dangers, and death."[51]

Alone, John Paton tearfully buried his family by hand. He labored on, a single man, bearing little fruit for decades to follow. On a return trip to Scotland, John married his second wife, Maggie. In 1866, the couple set sail for the island of Aniwa in the New Hebrides where in the midst of adversity they had a fruitful ministry. You can see why Paul tells us that you are best postured to advance God's kingdom in the face of opposition as a single person.

Even though we live in more Gospel-tolerant times,

---

[51] John Gibson Paton, *John G. Paton, Missionary to the New Hebrides* (London, Hodder and Stoughton, 1890), 130.

the church still faces persecution. Our headlines are filled with beheadings in the Mideast, hostages being taken in South America, and missionaries shot in Mexico. If you are considering God's call to the mission field, you might prayerfully ask if God hasn't gifted you with singleness. If you purpose to live your Christian life without compromise, fleshed out in radical proportions, you might well face the pains of persecution, ill health, and financial struggles where it is good to be single.

#2 – It Frees You from the Troubles of Marriage

Paul lists a second blessing that comes from a life of remaining single. The solitary life is free from the various troubles associated with marriage. Even though marriage is good and can lead to a life of joy, it still carries with it what Paul calls its own "trouble in the flesh" (v. 28). Many a single person has been tempted to reason, "If only I was married, then all of my problems would disappear." Wrong! Should you get married, a whole list of new problems are unleashed.

Marriage brings with it the double challenge of two lives joined together, each bringing their own unsanctified weaknesses. Even though you have been saved by the grace of God, you still must battle the flesh. The life of the best Christian is marked by varying degrees of selfishness, anger, pride, jealousy, and every other display of sin. When you marry, you become yoked together with another who struggles with the flesh for victory over sin. Then, should God bless you with children, you now add to the mix sinful children who are totally depraved. You now have what Paul calls, "trouble in the flesh." No wonder the Proverbs warn that it is "better to dwell in a corner of a housetop, than in a house shared with a contentious woman" (Proverbs 21:9). In other words, it is better to live alone than married with a spouse that breeds strife. Marriage never changes anything; it just intensifies everything you are and makes somebody else live with it.

As a single Christian growing in grace, you have trouble in the flesh—your own—but when you add a family, you may have "double trouble." Because marriage is the most intimate of relationships, it is also the most fragile and easily shattered. Even the best marriages are filled with hardships, conflicts, sacrifices, and compromises. No wonder marriage is one of the very means that God uses to sanctify us as a people.

#3 – It Means Unhindered Service to Christ

A third reason why singleness is a blessing is because "the time is short" (v. 29). In the original, the word that Paul uses for *time* (*kairos*) does not refer to chronological time, like the hours and minutes that are ticking away on a clock. Rather, it is better translated as "opportunities." Your opportune time to serve Christ is short. Your life is short! The return of Christ is imminent! We are quickly reaching the end, both biologically and eschatologically. Your opportunities that remain are few. Here's the principle: as your opportunities become more and more limited, your conduct should become more and more focused on the essentials.

What's Inside

Many years ago, a massive fire swept through Yellowstone National Park burning nearly 800,000 acres and making it the largest wildfire recorded in U.S. history. From our city's vantage point, the Beartooth Mountains to our east were a raging inferno. The smoke was so thick that the sun was reduced to a faint orange glow. Ash rained from the sky nonstop and accumulated on the cars like falling snow. However, our city was not facing any immediate danger. We felt a sense of safety and security with the 70 mile buffer that separated us from the flames, allowing life in Powell to continue unaffected.

However, things were different in Cooke City. This small Montana town found itself right in the pathway of the fire. A wall of flames advanced over the mountain burning out of control to within yards of the city. It was no longer life as usual; the opportunities for safety were running out quickly. You could smell the smoke, hear the crackling embers as pine trees exploded, and feel the intense heat.

A friend of mine was working on a ranch on the outskirts of Cooke City. He found himself suddenly overtaken by the advancing flames. This was not time for business as usual. It was no longer on his radar to mow the ranch house lawn, feed the horses, or catch up on the news. His opportunities were limited. He only had one last desperate hope for survival. As the flames were about to consume him, he took a running leap head first into a large watering pond. He desperately held his breath for what seemed like an eternity as the flames passed overhead. God was merciful that day and wonderfully spared my friend's life.

What's Inside

What a graphic picture of the spiritual state in which we find ourselves today. The sun is setting on this day of grace. There is little time left. Soon, "the clouds will be rolled back as a scroll; the trump shall resound, and the Lord shall descend…"! Even should Christ tarry, the sun is rapidly setting on your life. God has allotted the number of your days. Your Gospel opportunities are few! There is very little time left to proclaim the Gospel of Jesus Christ. As C.T. Studd so poetically penned it, "Only one life, 'twill soon be past, only what's done for Christ will last."

Kingdom opportunities are few. Therefore if you are married, "be as if not" (v. 29). Paul is not advocating divorce for the Gospel's sake. On the contrary, he is warning that you should not let your marriage keep you from your Christian service and devotion to God. Don't let your marital status dominate your life so as to keep you from seeking first His kingdom and righteousness.

Paul is giving you an urgent reminder to put aside everything that is passing away, including weeping, rejoicing, buying, worldly pleasure, and even marriage itself! Marriage will not continue in heaven. When the resurrection comes, there will no longer be any marriage (Mark 12:25). Christ will be your groom and you will be His bride forever! Therefore, do not become overly preoccupied with marriage.

Do you see the great Gospel advantages there are in being single? It's easier when you are single to live a passionate life of service for Christ. Why? You are not overly preoccupied with buying, selling, family sorrow, and worldliness. Therefore, invest your life in the furtherance of

God's kingdom! If you have been gifted with singleness, use it for kingdom purposes! Don't waste it on a life of self-centered sin. Remember, marriage is passing away.

#4 – It Allows for a Single Focused Life

Because the single Christian realizes that life is short and now is the time to lay aside all of life's distractions for the kingdom, the single life is freed up to be single-focused on service (vs. 32-35). In marriage, life as one flesh is a life committed to serving one another as husband and wife. The husband is the loving provider who must spend much of his time and strength working to keep the family going. As a husband and father, there seems like unending demand for me to supply my family with necessary resources.

I love my family, and it has been my passion to provide for all of their physical and spiritual needs. During the early years of church planting, this meant working two jobs to keep the Thomas boat afloat. Life began each morning with a gathering of the clan for family worship. We were one of the early pioneers in the homeschooling movement. We learned over the years what a huge sacrificial commitment this was. Although most of the daily teaching fell on my wife, I would fill in with Bible classes and electives like Greek. Our boys all loved playing basketball. An away game in Wyoming is not across town, but rather an overnighter across the state. The pressure to keep my family life in order finally resulted in my setting a limit on the number of times I would be away from my family each week to do ministry work. I limited myself to just two evenings a week. As a husband and dad, caring for my family is my primary calling, and it is a calling that has sometimes limited my availability to serve others.

The wife faces the same divided focus. Like the Proverbs 31 woman, she is lovingly serving her husband and children. She has so much to do and so little time to do it. She is the good wife who is up at "O dark thirty," preparing for the busy day ahead. You will find her shopping, cleaning the house, changing diapers, shuttling the kids to swimming lessons and soccer games. Like her husband, her focus is divided. Her time for service outside the home is limited. There is the dear sister in the hospital who needs to be visited. There are young ladies who recently trusted Christ who need to be discipled. So much to do and so little time to do it.

The married find their hearts divided between the heavenly and the earthly, the eternal and the temporal. They must rest knowing that they are to glorify God in their current station of life. This is the reality and sometimes frustration of being married. Paul is not saying these things to be critical of married life (v 35). Marriage is good! Rather, he is helping you see the added blessing of serving the Lord as a single person without distraction.

Here's the good news. The interests of the single believer are not divided. They are free to be single-focused on the things of God. The other evening I was leading a college Bible study. Following the study, a small group stayed after, filled with questions. Time flew by as we dug together into God's Word in search for answers. I looked down at my watch and it was almost midnight. I told the group, "I'm sorry guys, I have to bail out. My bride is at home waiting up for me!" That night I passed the teaching baton to a single seminary student who was free to continue to answer their questions until the wee hours of the night. He was blessed, being single, to be available to serve.

Jim, a dear friend, has faithfully pastored a multilingual church in the inner city of Los Angeles for more than 30 years. His gift of singleness has allowed him to serve in ways that few married pastors could. It doesn't matter the hour; he is always available by phone. Rather than coaching little league, he's involved in a multitude of ministries in a multilingual church. He has faithfully co-labored with the Korean speaking pastor. He continues to be active teaching the youth of the Spanish congregation. He brings the Word to the greying English-speaking body of believers. His undivided focus has been the administrative glue that has held these diverse congregations together.

Jim's ministry extends to the four corners of the world. His passport is well-stamped and always current. It is not unusual for him to get a call from a remote mission field asking if he can come and help. I have received his emails postmarked Korea, Columbia, Australia, Papua New Guinea, Turkey, Rome, Israel, and yes even some of the "uttermost" parts of the earth!

Don't be tempted to think that Paul is saying that there is some virtue in remaining single. Many single believers have wasted their lives on self-pleasure rather than offering their lives as living sacrifices to Jesus. Consider the great liberty you have for kingdom service.

You can:

- Devote much of your life to the reading of God's Word and to prayer without the interruption of caring for a spouse or bending to other family pressures.

- Live meagerly and use most of the resources that God graces you with to store up treasures in heaven.

- Take in people off the street and minister to them.

- Drop everything and go wherever God directs at a moment's notice.

- Be available to serve others whenever there is need.

Perhaps your heart has been stirred to ask, "How can I know if I have been gifted by God to a life of singleness?" This is a gift that will be evidenced by the grace to control one's sexual desire. Paul instructed his Corinthian readers, "But if they cannot contain (exercise sexual self-control), let them marry: for it is better to marry than to burn" (v. 9). Singleness is good, but it is better to marry than to burn with sexual desire. If your singleness continually inflames you with passionate sexual desires that continually tempt you to commit fornication, consider married life.

Perhaps you are asking God if it is His will that you remain single. One thing you do know for certain; today it is God's will for you to be in a non-married state. You must be careful to be thankful and not complain about God's sovereign provision. Don't be tempted to blame God for your own sexual sins. It's easy to cry out, "God, if you had

184

just given me a spouse, I would not have fallen into fornication." Remember, God promises to give you the grace and means to live a life of holiness in whatever state that His kind hand has placed you. No servant is greater than his Master (John 13:16). Our Lord lived out His earthly 33 years as a single man. Your temptation is no different than anyone else's, including Jesus. He promises to provide for you an avenue of escape so that you will be able to bear it (1 Corinthians 10:13). How much more will He gift His faithful followers with the strength to overcome inflamed sexual passions?

If you believe that you are gifted to a life of singleness, this does not always mean that it is God's will for you to remain single throughout your life. The gift of singleness is the only spiritual gift that I know of in the Scriptures that you have the option to use. If you are gifted to teach, you must teach! If you are gifted to give, you must give. But if you are gifted to be single, you have the freedom to remain single or get married. If you are single and desire to be married, you are free! You have not sinned (1 Corinthians 7:28). But if you do have the gift of singleness, I would encourage you for the kingdom's sake to faithfully use it.

In the opening chapters, we examined several questions: "Who should you marry?" and "how do you know God's will regarding the person you marry?" The short answer is that if you desire a blessed (happy) marriage, marry a blessed (happy) person. Settle for no one less than the person who bears the image of Jesus as revealed in the Beatitudes.

In this chapter, we stopped to ask an even more fundamental question: "Should you marry at all?" The life of discipleship is much bigger than marriage. It is a life of selfless obedience to Christ. The most fundamental question you can ask is: "How can I best live my life for the glory of God?" For many, it might include a life in a marriage. For those gifted with singleness, you are freed up to an undivided life of pursuing Christ!

Let me conclude with one final warning; be careful not to turn marriage into idolatry. Don't lift husband, wife, children, or even the institution of marriage itself on a totem pole above Christ. God is calling you to glorify Him whether married or single. May He alone be your ultimate delight!

Finally, I urge you not to close this book just yet. There is one chapter remaining—perhaps the most important chapter of all. Up to this point, we have been considering the marks of the *one* you are to consider in marriage. This last chapter is about *you*!

Chapter 15

Happy Are the Sure!

Test yourselves to see if you are in the faith; examine yourselves! Or do you not recognize this about yourselves, that Jesus Christ is in you— unless indeed you fail the test?

- 2 Corinthians 13:5 NASB

This book was written to help guide your path as you discern God's will regarding the person you are to marry. The guiding principle has simply been that a happy marriage is the blessing of marrying a happy person. As we saw in the first chapter, that must begin with an uncompromising commitment to be equally yoked. Marry a fellow believer! Sadly, many singles have fallen short by yielding to the temptation to rely on outside appearance and actions rather than taking a deep discerning look into the person's heart. This is where the Beatitudes become a great help. Jesus, in His sermon on the mount, lists the character qualities that will mark everyone who has been born from above. This is the person who is truly blessed or happy.

However, this can be a discouraging quest, causing some to bemoan, "What happened to all the godly single people? Have they all been added to the endangered species list?" That's a good question.

Part of the answer rests in the sad reality that there truly are few single Christians who are zealously committed to a life of godliness. It breaks my heart to see so many young, professing Christian men in their 20's still living with and supported by Mom and Dad. Vainly, they grew up singing, "Take My life and Let It Be." With their mouths they offered up their *moments, hands, feet, lips, silver, intellect, will, heart, and love.* Yet their time is now given over to entertainment. Their hands are glued to a video controller while their lips speak words of vanity because they are linked to a heart that loves this world.

Scarcity of godliness in others is only a part of the answer. You might be wondering, if it isn't a matter of scarcity, what is the real reason why I have never found that Christ-like believer?

The hard reality might be that the godly believer simply did not see the beauty of Christ in *you.*

If you were asked, who is a godly Christian looking to marry? Your answer might be, clearly, another godly believer. You would be right! Those whom are passionate about Christ will be attracted to others who share in that same passion. Could it be that God has brought beatitude-marked believers into your life, but they were repelled by your worldliness or self-centered focus? You must first be the person you desire to marry. A hollow testimony is not enough!

Listen carefully. Happiness in marriage will not come from marrying a Christian that bears the fruit of the Beatitudes. That's only one half of the happiness equation. To be equally yoked implies that both persons need to truly confess Christ. If happy marriages come from marrying a happy person, then it will only be true if both persons are truly blessed or happy.

Up to this point, our focus has been on discerning the heart of the other person. We mustn't stop there. There is still one more heart that must be known if you are to have a truly blessed marriage—your own! Let me encourage you to take up the mirror of God's Word and look carefully to see if your reflection bears the image of Jesus Christ.

You might object at this point, "Why do I need to look in the mirror? Of course I am a Christian. Why would I want to know God's will about marriage if I wasn't a Christian?" My reply is, "Don't be so quick to deny your need to look within before you look without." I have found over the years that there have been many young people who have been passionate about marrying a godly Christian whom seemed to display little more than a hollow profession of faith. They were like some of the little children in our churches who are unconverted and yet pray for their grandmas and grandpas to come to Christ. They see the need in others, but are still blind to their personal need to embrace the Cross of Jesus.

For some, it could well be that they are simply living out a Christian tradition. They were raised in a Christian family, grew up in the church, homeschooled, and were taught over and over again that they must not be unequally yoked. So they begin their pursuit of a future spouse in their church, college ministry, or Christian dating site without ever first seriously looking into their own heart.

For others, it might be the result of an over-confident faith where they actually profess more than they possess. These are the ones who give an outward profession of faith in Christ, but have never truly been born again. In Matthew 7, our Lord warns of the danger of being overly confident in your salvation. There were those who boasted of their spectacular ministry achievements who were shocked to discover they had no relationship with God at all. They were puffed up by their accomplishments and completely blind to their standing before God. Like many today, their hearts were deceived all the way up to judgment day when they heard the somber decree from the throne of God, "And then will I profess unto them, I never knew you: depart from me, ye that work iniquity" *(v. 23)*.

Then there are those who are truly saved, but are overly confident in the strength of their faith. They think they are a giant spiritual rock when in fact they are no more than a tiny spiritual pebble. We read, at the end of our Lord's last discourse and just hours away from His crucifixion, that the 11 joined together in one voice with a great profession of faith and full of assurance. They proudly confessed that Christ knows all things and was truly sent from God (John 16:30)! You might think that Jesus would have been filled with joy to hear such a grand confession at the end of His earthly ministry. Instead He asks, "Do ye now believe" (v. 31)? In other words, you think that your faith is so strong and yet you do not know that in just a few short hours you are going to abandon me and scatter for your lives. That's a question worthy of your self-examination. If you are professing faith in Christ, are you willing to answer our Lord's question, "Do you now believe?"

What's Inside

Do you know why it is so important to heed Paul's call to the professing Christian believers at Corinth to "Examine yourselves, whether ye be in the faith; prove your own selves. Know ye not your own selves, how that Jesus Christ is in you, except ye be reprobates" (2 Corinthians 13:5)? You must be willing to verify your own faith by examining your heart carefully to make sure your faith is true. A faith that J.C. Ryle describes as "16 ounces to the pound."

Are you willing to measure your faith by the same standard you measure the person you are considering in marriage? True saving faith will be marked by true spiritual fruit. As you look in the mirror of Scripture, do you see the foggy mist from an empty profession of faith or do you see a Spirit-filled heart that overflows in the beauty of the Beatitudes?

Let me encourage you to find a quiet place where you can get alone with God. Prayerfully ask the Holy Spirit to help you honestly answer the following soul-searching questions:

1. Do you have a credible testimony of faith in Jesus Christ? Notice, I purposely inserted the word, "credible." I didn't ask if you have a testimony. Rather, does your testimony bear the essential elements of repentance and faith in Jesus Christ as both Savior and Lord?

2. Are you poor in Spirit? Has God brought you to see your spiritual bankruptcy? Have you been humbled by God to see that your own good works are as filthy rags?

3. Have you been brought to mourn over your sin? Do you know that you have broken the holy law of God? Have you been graced to feel a deep sorrow for sinning against a holy God? Have you cried out for forgiveness with a willing desire to turn away from your sin?

4. Are you marked by meekness? Have you willingly put yourself under the rule of God in your life?

5. Do you hunger and thirst after righteousness? Do you know that the only righteousness that will avail you before almighty God is the righteousness of Christ? Do you have a thirst for the Word of God? A hunger for holiness? Is knowing Christ your supreme passion and delight?

6. Do you show mercy towards others? Do you see their hurts and needs and are you quick to reach out and alleviate their suffering? Do you feel the needs of sinners for salvation? Does it move you to reach out to them with the Gospel?

7. Are you pure in heart? Do you have an ongoing hatred for sin? Is it your passion for greater purity and Christ-likeness?

8. Are you a peacemaker? Is it your heart desire to bring the Gospel of peace to sinners? Do you pray for the souls of the lost and proclaim the Gospel to friends and loved ones who are lost?

9. Have you experienced the painful hand of persecution for righteousness sake? Have you experienced verbal or physical attacks for simply

living a Christ-like life before a fallen world?

A happy marriage is one of the great blessings that God bestows in this life, but in comparison it pales to the eternal happiness there is in being counted among the bride of Christ. Perhaps the Scriptures have brought you to discover that you have been falling short spiritually. Maybe you never have been brought to realize that the Christian faith is a transformational life that displays spiritual fruit that comes through trusting in Christ as Savior and Lord.

Perhaps God is awakening you to the reality that the faith you have been so confidently boasting in was nothing more than an empty religious shell filled with hot air. You now look back and see how you were quick to draw near to Christ with your lips, but your heart was far from Him. Like many, you were raised in a Christian home! Worshiped in a Christian church! Baptized as a Christian! Attended a Christian school! Hung out with Christian friends! Thought you were a Christian! But in your heart of hearts, you now realize that you were never truly converted. Do you realize what a wonderful place that is to find yourself in? You could have remained like all of the other religious hypocrites that are self-deceived into thinking that all was well with their souls only to hear Christ tell you on judgment day, "Depart from me, ye that work iniquity" (Matthew 7:23).

Here is the good news: now there is hope! Look to Christ. He is the only one who can save your soul. His shed blood alone can wash away all of your sins. His Gospel calls you to forsake your sins. Leave them all behind and come to Jesus! Trust in Him! Cast your whole being upon

Him! Deny yourself, pick up your means of martyrdom, and follow Christ as your Lord. He is a Savior that delights in saving sinners like you. Hallelujah! What a Savior!

For all who gazed carefully into the mirror of the Word and saw the beauty of the Beatitudes manifested in your life, you have much to be eternally thankful for. May God grace you with full assurance of His salvation. Use this season of singleness to plow deep into Christ. Immerse yourself in His Word, prayer and service. Prepare for marriage by learning what it means to be a Christian wife or husband.

It is my prayer that, by God's grace, you will reflect the image of the person you desire to marry. I pray that you will be the rare, rich jewel that will bring earthly, lifelong happiness to the one you marry and glory to your Heavenly Father!

Appendix 1

Pastoral Survey

I have been concerned as a pastor about the effect that our ever shifting culture has had on the faith and practice of the church. It seems like many churches today are all too ready to change their beliefs and practices to adjust to the signs of the time. I have seen, in my own lifetime, individual churches and denominations bow to the pressures from the feminist movement of the 60s, resulting in the modern egalitarian view of the role of women in the ministry. Sadly, we see the same trend as it relates to the family. As our culture continues to redefine marriage, it is not uncommon to find churches willingly conduct same-sex wedding ceremonies.

While writing this book, I became curious as to what the contemporary, mainstream church's understanding was of the father's role in overseeing the courtship of his daughter. I wanted to know how the churches were interpreting and applying 1 Corinthians 7:36-38. Has the giving of a daughter's hand by her dad become mere formalism or does a father still have authority over his daughter when it comes to the matter of courtship?

I decided to frame a questionnaire that I would send out to a broad cross-section of evangelical pastors. This survey was not meant to be a scientific study. Rather, it was one pastor's attempt to simply take the pulse of other churches. The survey contained 7 questions. I encouraged the pastors to feel free to add their own additional comments.

Results of the Survey

I sent this survey to more than 1,500 pastors of independent evangelical churches and Protestant denominations. I must admit that I was slightly disappointed by the less than 10% response. However, I believe the responses that I did receive helped shed some light on the current understanding of the broad spectrum of the evangelical church today.

1. Does a Christian father today have authority over whom his Christian daughter marries?

    - Yes – 73%
    - No – 27%

    a. If "yes," does this authority continue over self-supporting Christian daughters living on their own?

        - Yes – 53%
        - No – 47%

    b. If "yes," when does this authority end?

        - When the daughter leaves home – 33%
        - When the daughter turns 18 – 16%
        - Upon the daughter's marriage – 36%
        - Other – 18%

2. Which of the following are proper matters for the
    father to consider as he exercises this authority?

    a. The man's salvation (unequally yoked
        relationship):

        • Yes – 100%

    b. Other scripturally mandated qualifications?

        • Yes – 94%
        • No – 6%

        If "yes" to (b), please check which ones:

        • Ability to support wife – 81%
        • Ability to spiritually lead wife and
          family – 84%
        • Practical personal holiness – 92%
        • Members of a local church – 65%
        • Unbiblical divorce – 55%
        • Doctrinal unity – 40%

    c. Are there other practical matters that would
        cause the father to conclude that the
        marriage would be unwise?

        • Yes – 88%
        • No – 12%

        If "yes" to (c), please check which one(s):

        • Respect for others in authority – 64%
        • Type of employment – 45%
        • Age differences – 47%
        • Other – 48%

3. Does a daughter's refusal to submit to her father's authority in this area of marriage rise to the level of sin?

   - Yes – 60%
   - No – 40%

   If "yes," should this be made a matter of church discipline?

   - Yes – 52%
   - No – 48%

   If "no," what are the proper consequences, if any, if a couple continues to pursue marriage contrary to the father's expressed will?

   - None – 50%
   - Take all steps to reach the daughter's conscience – 98%
   - Other – 56%

4. If a couple does get married contrary to the father's will, what should be the ongoing nature of their relationship to their Christian parents? (Check any or none.)

   - Unconditional forgiveness – 48%
   - Fractured relationship—forgiveness and reconciliation subject to the couple's repentance – 30%
   - Withdrawal of father's blessing (Does not give her hand in marriage) – 32%
   - Church discipline – 10%
   - Other – 18%

5. Does a Christian father have any authority over the man who continues to see his daughter contrary to his denied permission to court her?

  • Yes – 45%
  • No – 55%

6. Does this man's actions, contrary to the father's will, rise to the level of a sin issue?

  • Yes – 67%
  • No – 33%

7. Should this be pursued as a matter of church discipline?

  • Yes – 45%
  • No – 55%

Reflecting on the Results

I was encouraged to see that more than 70% of the pastors surveyed interpreted 1 Corinthians 7:36-38 to mean that the father has God-given authority over whom his daughter courts and ultimately marries. However, as you read through the survey, you quickly see how this authority is to be exercised is open to broad interpretation. The pastors surveyed are almost evenly divided over whether or not this authority terminates with adulthood. With an increasing number of young people delaying marriage past college into adulthood, this becomes an important question for fathers to wrestle with.

As I mentioned earlier, the Bible does not directly

address adult, single women living independently of their parents. Wisdom would dictate that a good father should exercise his headship over his adult, single daughter differently than his young, single daughter living at home. However, a daughter's need for fatherly protection, wisdom, and guidance in discerning a suitor's qualifications does not terminate on her 18th birthday.

This survey is not meant to be used as ammunition to support or refute any particular point of view. It is only meant to be a reflection of the current understanding of the father's role by some evangelical churches. Only the Spirit-enlightened exposition of the Word of God can direct us into right understanding of a father's role. May Jesus strengthen His church with a fresh resolve to faithfully apply His Word in our families, especially when it stands in complete opposition to the world around us.

Appendix 2

Digging Deeper

In chapter 2, "Paternal Protection," 1 Corinthians 7:36-38 is offered as a proof text for God granting to the father the authority to oversee his daughter's courtship. If you opened your own copy of the English Standard Version or New International Version you might have been surprised to discover it describing the relationship between an engaged man and his fiancée. However, for those of you reading a King James Version, New King James Version, or New American Standard Version you would read of the relationship between a father and his daughter. Which is correct? I thought it would be profitable to dig a little deeper into this passage to not only discover its meaning but also its proper application in our families.

This difficult passage has given rise to the following three views:

1. The engaged couple view. This has been summarized as follows: "A young man is engaged to a young woman; because of social conditions they have decided as yet not to marry. But the physical pressures are becoming too great for the young man. Now Paul counsels the man to seek marriage as a solution to the dilemma he and his virgin are facing. Paul assures the man that in doing so he is not sinning. If the person is able to

control himself and decides to postpone marriage, Paul approves of this decision." [52]

2. The "spiritual marriage" view. This unusual view describes a man and a woman who live together in "spiritual harmony" but refrain from any sexual union. They seek a union of spirit but not of bodies. In the event that the man cannot sexually control himself, Paul advises them to marry, but if he can control himself then he should remain unmarried, which is better.[53]

3. The father of a virgin daughter view. John MacArthur best summarizes this view, "In light of the extant teaching about the advantages of singleness, some of the fathers in Corinth apparently had dedicated their young daughters to the Lord as permanent virgins. But when the daughters became of marriageable age, many of them no doubt wanted to be married, and their fathers were in a quandary. Should they break the vow they made for the girl? It is likely that many of the girls did not have the gift of singleness and were struggling with their desire to get married and their desire to please their fathers and the Lord. The problem was among those mentioned in the church's letter to Paul (7:1).

Again the emphasis is on the option believers have in regard to marriage. If the intended partner is a Christian, marriage is always permissible. A father

[52] Simon Kistemaker, *New Testament Commentary, 1 Corinthians*, (Grand Rapids, MI: Baker Academic, 2007), 254.
[53] Consult Roland Seboldt, *Spiritual Marriage in the Early Church: A Suggested Interpretation of 1 Corinthians 7:36-38*, ConcThMonth 30 (1959): 103-19;176-89.

who had vowed his daughter's remaining single in order to serve the Lord more devotedly was free to change his mind and allow her to marry if she were insistent. After all, it was a vow made for someone else, and was therefore subject to the person's spiritual needs. **If she should be of full age, and if it must be so, let them do what he wishes, he does not sin; let her marry.** Just as unmarried people themselves are under no restraint (v. 35) and do not commit sin by marrying (v. 28), neither does a father who has made a vow do wrong by changing his mind. His making the vow is good; but if his daughter is not able or inclined to follow it, both she and her father are fee to do as they wish. **If it must be so** indicates that she really is designed for marriage, and the father should allow it.

But if the father **stands firm in his heart**, that is, does not change his mind about the promise; and is **under no constraint** by the daughter to change his mind; and has a good and pure motive (**has authority over his own will**) and is deeply committed (**decided this in his own heart**); he may **keep his own virgin daughter.** **Constraint** is better translated 'necessity,' referring to the daughter's necessity to get married.... Only the daughter's unwillingness to keep the vow should cause the father to change his mind. His steadfastness in his vow will encourage his daughter to be steadfast in hers. In doing that **he will do well**.

Paul repeats the option: **So then both he who gives his own virgin daughter in marriage does well, and he who does not give her in marriage will do better.**"[54]

This is the traditional view held by such commentators as: John Calvin, Matthew Henry, John Gill, Leon Morris, and John MacArthur.

As you can see this short passage can lend to more than one interpretation. Which view is correct? I join the many conservative commentators who reject the spiritual marriage view. A couple living together celibate is a bizarre view that not only places a couple in the position of extreme temptation but fails to avoid the appearance of evil. Leon Morris raises the following decisive objection to this view, "Paul regards the withholding of sexual relations by married people an act of fraud (v. 5; few of those holding this position discuss this point). It may be done by mutual consent 'for a time,' and the couple must then 'come together again.' It is impossible to think that a man who valued the sex act in marriage so highly would acquiesce in a situation where it was done away with." [55]

Of the two remaining views I support the third view of the father of the virgin daughter, also commonly referred to as the "traditional view." I will do my best to unpack my reasons without becoming too technical.

[54] John MacArthur, *The New Testament Commentary, 1 Corinthians,* (Chicago, IL: Moody Publishers, 1984), 185-186.
[55] Leon Morris, *1 Corinthians. Tyndale New Testament Commentaries,* (Downers Grove, IL: Intervarsity Press, Reprint 2008), 119.

One of the difficulties of the young man and his virgin fiancée view is that you must read into this passage our modern understanding of engagement. Morris notes, "The Greeks do not appear to have had an 'engagement' at all (Conzelmann). There was a betrothal among the Jews and the Romans, but this was more than our 'engagement'; it was in effect marriage, stage 1, and could be broken only by divorce proceedings. And it was not brought about by an agreement of the couple; it was an arrangement made by the parents."[56]

Context. Verse 36 does not appear to introduce a new subject of a young man who is engaged to a young fiancée or a "spiritual marriage." Paul is continuing with his original thought from verse 25, "now concerning virgins." The following verses (vv. 25-38) are about "virgins" (unmarried daughters). Verse 28 speaks of those daughters that are already betrothed and verse 36 speaks to fathers who are considering the proper course of action in how to lead their daughters in marriage.

In the broader context this view is consistent with all of the biblical passages cited in chapter 2 of this book which speak of the father's prerogative to give the hand of his daughter in marriage. It is also exemplified by Jephthah in Judges 11:30-41 who made a vow to dedicate his daughter to the Lord and never give her to be married.

Grammar. A quick gaze through these three verses and you will discover that they are pregnant with pronouns, "he," "himself," "she," "her," and "them." A proper understanding of this passage requires connecting these

---

[56] Ibid., 119.

pronouns with their antecedents. All of the female pronouns seem to refer to the "virgin" (KJV, NKJV, NIV) or "betrothed" (ESV). Each of the male pronouns refers back to "man" (KJV, NASB, and NIV) or "anyone" (ESV).

Who is this "virgin?" Paul uses the same word "virgin" (*parthenos*) throughout this chapter (vv. 28, 34, 36-38). It would seem likely that he would be speaking of the same group of young ladies not variable groups. This consistency of use best fits daughters who were unmarried. A common objection is "his virgin" is not a common phrase for "his daughter." However, Morris does find the following support for this meaning, "(but it does occur; LSJ cites Sophocles as saying 'my virgins' for 'my daughters')."[57]

Paul further describes her as a virgin daughter who is "past the flower of her youth" (*hyperakmos*). This can mean past marriageable age. In Calvin's day the law defined the age of marriage as somewhere between 12 and 20 years of age.[58] Paul is describing a virgin daughter who is past the age when marriage would be expected. This understanding necessitates the "man" Paul is addressing in verse 36 to be the father of his unmarried daughter.

Another important piece of the puzzle that further clarifies that Paul is speaking to a father rather than a fiancé is his use of the verb "giving in marriage" (*gamizo*) (v. 38). Paul does not use this verb anywhere else in his writings except twice in verse 39. Paul chooses to use *gamizo*

---

[57] Ibid., 118.
[58] John Calvin, *Calvin's Commentaries vol. XX, The Epistles to the Corinthians vol. 1* (Grand Rapid, MI: Baker, reprinted 1981), 265.

("giving in marriage") instead of *gameo* ("to marry"). Seven other places in this chapter Paul uses the word *gameo* ("to marry"), instead of *gamizo*. Why would Paul change verbs without intending to change their meanings? It seems clear that by the use of *gamizo* Paul is speaking of a father who is giving his daughter in marriage.

Conclusion: Of the three views above I embrace the third one of a father exercising God-given paternal authority over his virgin daughter in matters of marriage. Some of the modern commentators reject this view because of the ancient culture of Paul's day which practiced arranged marriages. They steer away from this father of a virgin daughter view fearing the potential Pandora's Box it might open in our modern cultural understanding of marriage. Kistemaker, who holds to the fiancé of an engaged young lady admits, "Nevertheless, difficulties surround the third (fiancé of an engaged young lady view) explanation, because we tend to interpret the text within our own culture and times." [59]

I believe we can come to a proper understanding of the teachings of Paul within the context of the culture of his day and draw out those practical principles that transcend customs and times. Arranged marriages are neither commanded nor condemned in the Bible. Such ancient customs of a father choosing a spouse or vowing to keep a daughter a perpetual virgin are clearly out of sync with twenty-first century America. The abiding principle of this passage, as well as many others found throughout the Bible, is the role of parents, particularly the father, to give

---

[59] Kistemaker, *New Testament Commentary, 1 Corinthians,* 254.

his daughter in marriage. This paternal prerogative is so broadly taught in Scripture that it remains standing in spite of how one ultimately interprets this passage. Today, this "giving" includes the faithful discharge of protecting the purity of his daughter during courtship along with the necessary spiritual vetting of the suitor so that on her wedding day when the pastor asks, "Who gives this woman to be married to this man?" her father can respond with a whole-hearted "I do!"

What's Inside

About the Author

Donald Thomas, is the pastor-teacher of Trinity Bible Church in Powell, Wyoming. He received a Master's Degree from Talbot Theological Seminary and a J.D. from John Marshall Law School. He practiced law in California and served as a professor at the Simon Greenleaf School of Law. He and his wife Mary have seven grown children and seventeen grandchildren.

Made in the USA
Middletown, DE
14 May 2015